ABOVE SAN DIEGO

by ROBERT CAMERON

A new collection of historical and original
aerial photographs of San Diego

with text by
NEIL MORGAN

CAMERON and COMPANY, San Francisco, California

Tourmaline Beach near Pacific Beach.

Captions on Page 160.

(opposite) Coronado Bridge over San Diego Harbor.

TABLE OF CONTENTS

Such a book as this does not reach publication without more than the usual amount of cooperation from many people. So, for their encouragement and expertise, I thank the following:

Hatsuro Aizawa, Joyce Albers, Anthony Cameron, Todd Cameron, George Croom, Sharon Croom, Alison Da Rosa, Dwight Donatto, John Goy, Tina Hodge, Al JaCoby, Robert Maldonado, Dulcie Molyneux, Judith Blakely Morgan, Patricia O'Grady, Sandra Roberts, William A. Shaw Jr., Linda Shaw, Bob Witty, Charmaine Wong, Robert H. Wornhoudt.

and especially pilots:
David Gibbs,

and for special aerial research and piloting, Alan Kappmeier.

Credit for Historical Photographs:
San Diego Historical Society
Los Angeles Public Library

CAMERON and COMPANY

Pier 23   The Embarcadero   San Francisco   CA 94111-1136   415/777-5582   800/779-5582   Fax 415/777-4814

Library of Congress Catalog Number: 90-81498
ABOVE SAN DIEGO ISBN 0-918684-24-2
© 1990 by Robert W. Cameron and Company, Inc. All rights reserved.

First Printing, 1990
Second Printing, 1991
Third Printing, 1996
Fourth Printing, 2000
Fifth Printing, 2000

Book design by
JANE OLAUG KRISTIANSEN

Color processing by The New Lab, San Francisco and Chrome Lab, San Diego
Camera work by Color Comp Graphics, San Francisco
Photo Retouching by Alicemarie Matrux and Jerome Vloeberghs, San Francisco
Color Separations and Printing by Dai Nippon Printing Co., Hong Kong

ABOVE SAN DIEGO INTRODUCTION
by Neil Morgan

I first saw the book *Above London* during Christmas week of 1980 as I reveled, earthbound, in the sidewalks and streets of that city. At Foyle's, that creaky warren of books, the jacket photograph reached out and grabbed me. There was the Royal Naval College at Greenwich, as I always imagine it but never quite find it: austere and romantic, symmetric, alone, set apart in time, just as Palladio and Inigo Jones and Sir Christopher Wren must have intended.

I had not yet met Bob Cameron then, nor heard of his way with Pentax, gyroscope, and helicopter. But the words of the book were from Alistair Cooke, a man of impeccable alliances. I bought it instantly as though it were my only chance, and lugged it home to California.

Since then Bob Cameron's books have reversed my long aversion to aerial photography. I have been taking pictures, sometimes seriously, since I was a boy, and to me, aerials were faceless maps. But Bob confirms the caveat we learn from travel, from all of life: our rewards rise as we invest more of ourselves. He is a clever and indefatigable photographer, but much more: a literate, thinking man who uses his camera to share his own prejudices and perceptions. It seems extraordinary to me that he can show us how he feels about the world's great cities in portfolios of photographs that are essentially without people. His cities are dazzling, sometimes damning evidence of who their people are, what their priorities have been, and how they have chosen to live.

In the case of San Diego, Bob Cameron's vision is an astonishment even to a writer who has spent much of forty years in chronicling the city. For me, part of the pleasure of our collaboration was in seeking out visuals that tell even more than they show: insights on the minds and hearts of the people of San Diego, their passions and eccentricities, their styles and standards or lack of them, and the devious ways in which they have sought to manage their environment. That final revelation is crucial evidence. San Diego is a city of migrants who have adopted the setting. There are few large cities so dominated by those who have voluntarily moved from another place. Many came to San Diego because they admired its space and pace. Yet by coming they altered both, and created the political issue that has become dominant: the control of growth.

Just as we study Rome through its roads and viaducts, we draw a hint of what San Diegans are thinking from their water pipelines, snaking for hundreds of miles across desert and mountains, and from the intricate web of freeways that bisects mesa and canyon, divides cities, and creates a mobile, restless, and often rootless society. We understand more by seeing what San Diegans have done with their harbors and beaches.

There is a natural harbor from which cargo is strangely absent; its shores diverted to marinas, lagoons, beaches, yacht clubs, resorts, restaurants, research laboratories and new towns. We see a conglomerate of communities that fronts on the Pacific Ocean and tails back to coastal mountains: the tiered scale of status in the leisure worship that is fancied to be inherent in America's sunset shore.

We find malls rising like little downtowns, a Californian version of community centers for shopping, dining, entertainment, and public forum.

We look down on bulldozers leveling dusty suburban hillsides for new towns, and the fields of outdoor nurseries that provide instant landscaping for those towns. We trace some of the canyons around which San Diego has grown, arteries of natural open space that pump airiness into older residential neighborhoods.

Gazing down into spacious estates in the privileged enclaves of San Diego, and into neighborhoods blighted by drugs and crime, we ponder the great divides of our cities, accentuated in San Diego by its natural beauty and acquired prosperity.

A photograph taken along the international border between Tijuana and San Diego, the two largest cities of the long border between our two nations, explains a collision of cultures and economics that is at once San Diego's agony and its window of opportunity. We see a boundary between two societies that is almost painful in its contrasts, as clear and sharp as if it were a line drawn by an artist.

It is possible through these photographs to track the beginnings of San Diego, which were also the beginnings of modern California, and to follow the city's meandering evolution from a Spanish pueblo to an insular, transplanted Midwestern town by the sea, to a Navy city, and on to its present rich diversity. The migrants of this generation have been a refreshing new breed, and they have superimposed on old San Diego their demanding visions of present and future. It remains a hugely livable city. But San Diego has become more: a threshold city that has not yet passed its point of no return. It is a magnet for innovators in science and technology, and for those who envision America's future in the Pacific basin.

I have written books about San Diego, and edited others, and I am somewhat startled to conclude that Bob Cameron's beautiful volume may come to serve as the most useful single book about this fluid and complex city. From the altitudes at which Bob Cameron works his spell, above the human hubbub, issues and answers seem clearer. It seems easier to decide just what is going right or wrong.

THE OUTER SHORELINE

Beside the beach where San Diego and Orange counties meet, about sixty miles northwest of San Diego Harbor, Southern California Edison Co. operates San Onofre Nuclear Generating Station. Its a veteran: Its first generator went into service in 1968. Three reactors can produce 2,625 megawatts of electricity, one-fifth of the company's electrical load for the 50,000-square-mile Southern California region that ranges from Kern County to San Diego. To many San Diegans, Southern California Edison, based at Rosemead near Los Angeles, has become a symbol of the dreaded megalopolis at their north. San Diego-born businesses have often been sold out in mergers, with corporate headquarters leaving the city, sometimes for Los Angeles. In a bitter merger battle that climaxed in 1991, Southern California Edison failed in its bid to acquire San Diego Gas & Electric Co.

(opposite) Man-made harbors like these two at Oceanside have become pivotal in Southern California's development: navigable havens along a desert coast. San Diego is built around a natural harbor; but most others, including giant Los Angeles Harbor, are man-made. So is Oceanside Harbor, center, which was dedicated in 1963, when pleasure boating was becoming as common as golfing among San Diegans. Much of the harbor site was deeded by the Marine Corps, which operates the adjacent Camp Pendleton, including its own boat basin, at bottom. The base, still mostly rangeland, provides a 17-mile-long buffer along San Diego County's north coast. It is the whimsy of San Diegans that Camp Pendleton holds back the overflowing tide of Los Angeles growth and maintains San Diego as a snug cul-de-sac.

Few oceanfront homesites remain empty along the San Diego County coast, and their prices are discussed in awed whispers. Early migrants tended to avoid the oceanfront and to build homes on drier, sunnier sites, away from mildew and coastal fogs. But with later migrants from middle America and Europe, oceanfront living acquired the cachet of the ultimate. There are drawbacks. At Solana Beach, left, waves and wind have caused cliff erosion that encroaches on front yards and finally undermines house foundations. At Encinitas, right, sea walls are used to diminish tidal impact, and steep stairways are built on the face of nearly vertical sandstone cliffs between home and beach.

At Del Mar, clifftside estates overlook both the ocean and the sandy delta of the San Dieguito River, one of the San Diego rivers that, for most of each year, are sand beds. Thoroughbred trainers, fond of the racetrack "where the turf meets the surf," claim therapeutic powers for this confluence of riverbed and beach. During the track meeting, from July to just past Labor Day, Del Mar exercise boys walk horses from stables through the sand to strengthen their ankles in shallow seawater. Bing Crosby and Pat O'Brien launched the track in 1937, providing a site for the county fair that was their cover story, and it was all done in the name of California's 22nd Agricultural District. In time Lucille Ball and Desi Arnaz became familiar faces at the racetrack, and kept a beach home

nearby. Their friend Jimmy Durante was a neighbor and a track regular too. J. Edgar Hoover and Clyde Tolson had their box during vacation weeks while old-boy Texas millionaires Sid Richardson and Clint Murchison owned the track in the name of Boys Clubs. Opening day in July along the corridors and behind the glass walls of the directors' box at the Turf Club, remains a startling parade of movieland fashion and chutzpah, with huddled talk of deals. The track's general manager is Joe Harper, with his own showbiz connection: he's a grandson of Cecil B. DeMille. But at Del Mar political talk can override showbiz; one of the more devoted of track regulars is Robert Strauss, who interrupted his 1991 stay at Del Mar to become U. S. ambassador to the Soviet Union at the time of the coup.

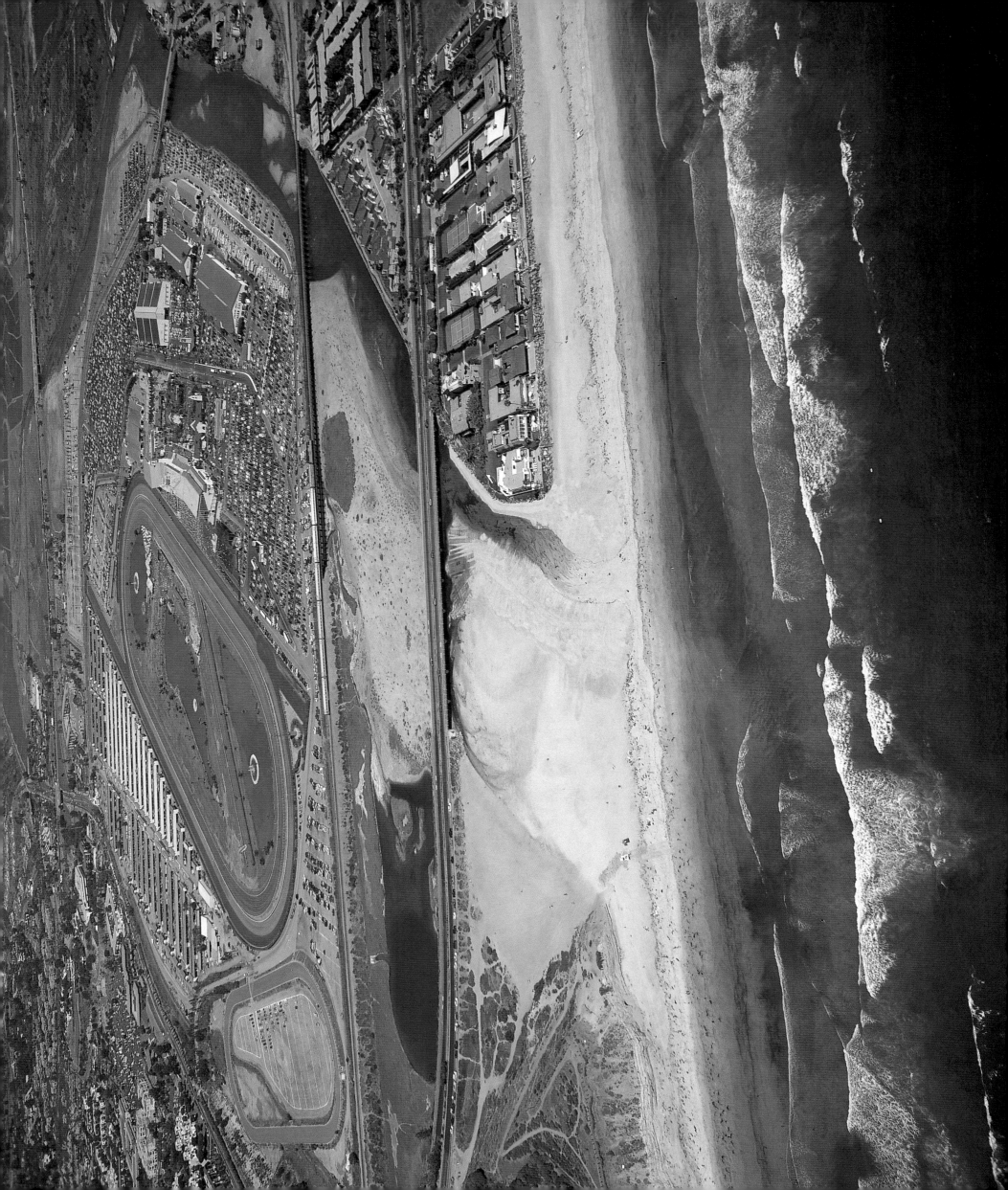

(*opposite*) La Jolla Shores is part of a seventy-mile system of public ocean beaches that attracts visitors to San Diego from all over the country and the world. Kellogg Park, the grassy area above the beach, is an outpost of public access. Many of the homes along the terraces above sell, if offered, well into seven figures. But student oceanographers from nearby Scripps Institution still take advantage of their lunch breaks to dart from laboratories and plunge with their surfboards into the sea.

The annual San Diego Open is played over two municipal golf courses, built beside the site of Camp Callan, an army base in World War II. These courses are part of a startling profusion: more than fifty public and private golf courses in San Diego County. This cliffside had been city-owned land since the Mexican era. Much of it has been zoned for science research, such as that going on in the ivory-hued buildings of Scripps Clinic and Research Foundation, designed by Edward Durrell Stone (mid-right). Just beyond is the Sheraton Grande Torrey Pines Hotel.

Scientists from this campus of Scripps Institution of Oceanography roam the world defining currents and tides, pursuing warming trends and greenhouse effects. It became a part of the University of California in 1912 with the benevolence of Ellen Browning Scripps, the maiden half-sister of newspaper publisher E. W. Scripps, who settled on a ranch at nearby Miramar. In 1960 this graduate school, the world's oldest and largest center of marine science research, became the core of the newborn University of California at San Diego. The oceanographers' long pier, a La Jolla landmark, begins at lower left. Scripps's fleet of four oceanographic research vessels and two floating platforms makes up the largest component of the U.S. academic fleet.

Architect Louis Kahn's contribution to the San Diego landscape was Jonas Salk's research institute above the cliffs of Torrey Pines Mesa. It has served as laboratory and retreat for Nobel laureates like Renato Dulbecco, its director in 1990, and the mathematician Jacob Bronowski, known most widely for his television series, "The Ascent of Man." Funded in 1960 by the March of Dimes, soon after Salk had developed his polio vaccine, this stark castle of teak and concrete shelters biological sciences research in cancer, birth defects, growth deficiencies, virus infections, memory loss, and AIDS. In his mid-seventies, Salk inhabits a top-floor aerie of bleached oak and concrete, looking out to sea past walls hung with canvases painted by his wife, Francoise Gilot, the most literate of Picasso's women. An addition approved in 1991 was to be built among trees at bottom of picture.

If there is a sensory core of La Jolla, it is the La Jolla Beach and Tennis Club. Many of the greatest tennis players of three generations have played on these courts. But it is the passion of club members and summer guests for splendid anonymity that helps to give La Jolla some reputation for buttoned-down propriety. By Eastern or European standards, the club is *nouveau*. In 1926, when members of the founding Kellogg family were still just summer visitors, cows grazed on the site. Free bus service from San Diego and hucksters' free lunches lured prospective members, and they were promised a yacht club. That dream foundered over the cost of breakwaters. No matter. Today there are 14 tennis courts, 89 apartments, and a two-year waiting list for membership. Others may dine in the public Marine Room, where high tides crash against thick plate-glass windows that haven't always held back the sea. Or they may buy tickets, if they're swift, to dance on the tennis courts in August at the Jewel Ball, San Diego's glitziest gala.

(*opposite*) Town and gown merge along this La Jolla cliff. Jonas Salk and Walter Munk, one of the most honored of Scripps oceanographers, have homes near the top left corner of this photograph. A non-academic neighbor on the precipice uses a funicular to visit his round beach house. The large building houses the Southwest Fisheries Center and National Marine Fisheries Service, whose vessels roam the oceans; one returned from Antarctica in 1989, its steel railings bent by the storms of Cape Horn. Offshore here, a submarine canyon drops off with such sheer precipices that divers compare it with the Grand Canyon. Now Scripps research extends into space; former astronaut Sally Ride directs the University of California Space Institute headquartered here. But it is the Scripps aquarium that draws public crowds.

(opposite) Only two condominium towers break the height limits that now prevail in La Jolla. They are monuments to the 1960s, when developers sensed the drawing power of "the village" and caught civic planners dozing in the sun. Nothing towering is built in La Jolla any longer. For years after its beginnings in the 1880s, La Jolla's unofficial town limits extended up the slopes of Mount Soledad and stopped. Now communities on all sides of Soledad brandish the name. Legal precedent sustains them. When Scripps Memorial Hospital prepared to expand from central La Jolla to a larger site miles to the northeast, a judge was required to define the boundaries of La Jolla. Solomon-like, he ruled that La Jolla was nothing more than a state of mind without official boundaries. With that, he opened thousands of parched inland acres to subdividers' hyperbole: communities with ingenious interweavings of the name of La Jolla.

The Seville, one of those two outsized condominium towers, casts a shadow across the 18th tee toward La Jolla Country Club. This golf course is remarkable for its prodigal use of ocean-view acres at the center of the community. The first nine holes were built on land bought from the city of San Diego in 1913; the second nine were added in 1927. The initiation fee was set that year at $200, annual dues were $90. With a new clubhouse, the Country Club usurped the social role of the oceanfront hotel Casa de Manana, later to become a church-owned retirement home. Golf professionals who grew up on this course include Gene Littler, Craig Stadler, Mickey Wright, Chuck Courtney, Phil Rodgers, and John Schroeder. By 1989, the club had 420 golfing members, a wait list of more than 70, and a buy-in fee of about $60,000.

That other condo high-rise of La Jolla, 939 Coast, stacks up above the sea at left. The low buildings at center are the Casa de Mañana, where some of the more fortunate retired look out on Children's Pool. At the top of Jenner Street are a Hard Rock Cafe and Sharper Image and a clutch of art galleries, aimed like most of Prospect Street's boutiques at the strolling visitor. Bells toll in the tower of the very-Anglican St. James-by-the-Sea Episcopal Church at far right, across the street from the San Diego Museum of Contemporary Art. Much of La Jolla is named for Ellen Browning Scripps; the museum was built around her old home. John Cole's Book Shop, a village landmark, occupies the Scripps garden cottage.

(opposite) Even in San Diego, a city rich with parks and open space, Ellen Browning Scripps Park at the center of La Jolla is exceptional for its setting. La Jolla Cove is at the far left, and La Jolla Bay above it. Coast Walk is a public footpath that winds along the cliff across the front yards of oceanfront homes. Above the park (just right of center) is La Valencia Hotel, a 1920s treasure with red tile roofs, pink turret and Mediterranean ambiance. Some consider it the last appropriate structure to have risen in La Jolla.

Neptune Place winds down toward the ocean and turns with the shoreline toward Windansea Beach, the surfers' favorite. A San Diego mayor, Maureen O'Connor, owned an oceanfront home close by; so did the U.S. protocol officer William F. Black, a noted La Jollan, and the late Gene Klein, who sold the San Diego Chargers football franchise and bought racehorses that won more often.

(opposite) At the corner where La Cañada reaches shoreward from La Jolla Boulevard and turns into Camino de la Costa is Sun Gold Point. The name, chosen by an early real estate subdivider, is one to which most of the neighborhood remains happily oblivious. More familiar is the California bungalow that wraps itself around the corner just above. The English-born mystery novelist Raymond Chandler, author of *The Big Sleep*, lived here from 1947 until shortly before his death in 1959. He was stubbornly reclusive except for brief outbursts when he assaulted La Jolla as the home of "barren old women and arthritic billionaires." One night after his wife's death, drunk and depressed, he fired two shots into a shower ceiling here, and was rushed off to County Hospital's psycho ward. I picked him up there the next morning and drove him to a private hospital for a dry-out. Chandler gave me a sort of tip: In *The Long Goodbye*, Philip Marlowe was driven home one night by a reporter named Lonnie Morgan.

At the time of Pearl Harbor in 1941, La Jolla Hermosa was a rich man's subdivision with lonely open spaces. The big house with the oceanfront swimming pool had recently been completed. It was shunned by panicky investors. Japanese submarines were reported offshore. Californians feared they would be the next Japanese target. Camouflage nets rose over the Consolidated aircraft plant, and blackouts were ordered. Real estate prices collapsed. Four years later, in London, Jack Vietor, an Army Air Corps flier just released from the Nazi POW camp at Stalag Luft, saw an ad for this home in Town and Country magazine.

The asking price was $100,000; he cabled an offer for $96,000 and got it. Through the 1960s and 1970s, as Vietor became publisher of San Diego Magazine, the world's best backgammon players gathered here for an annual tournament known as the Vietor Cup. The legendary Barclay Cooke, a Yalie, an opera fanatic and author of "The Cruelest Game," was a perennial winner. There were matches when more money changed hands than when Vietor had bought the house. Today, the vacant lots are gone, and so is Vietor. His heirs put the house on the market in 1989 for $8 million.

More masochism for what-if browsers: This photograph was taken above La Jolla in 1921, looking northeast. Oceanfront cliffs are at the bottom. The ravine, largely filled in today, relates to Ravina Street. The campus at the center is The Bishop's School, La Jolla's most exclusive private school, then twelve years old. On beyond is La Jolla Recreation Center, where tennis was as much an obsession in 1921 as today. At the far left is La Jolla Women's Club, one of several charming examples of Irving Gill architecture in San Diego. The picture at right is blocks to the south, in the Gold Coast of Camino de la Costa, with the Vietor house at far right. Corporate executives favor this oceanfront; homes are owned by such as Forrest Shumway, long with Allied-Signal; Richard Cramer, founder of IMED; and Michael Dingman, who founded and directs The Henley Group. Tides collide along the Gold Coast in a maelstrom of cross-currents and white froth, breaking over offshore rocks with each sharp turn in the shoreline. Floodlights make the scene a theatrical backdrop for dinner parties.

West-facing sandstone cliffs turn golden at sunset along San Diego's oceanfront. These are in the neighborhood known as Sunset Cliffs. On the seaward flank of Point Loma, Sunset Cliffs is more affordable than La Jolla and captures some of the same Riviera mystique. Sunset Cliffs people consider themselves more old-line San Diego, more likely to endow the Zoo than La Jolla Playhouse, more prone to spend a winter weekend on horseback in the San Diego mountains than beside a pool at Palm Springs.

(opposite) Bird Rock is part of La Jolla, but its residents endure nicknames like Baja La Jolla, where Pacific Beach begins, it was, for decades, a neighborhood where the less affluent might hope to get their first hint of La Jolla living. The bungalow I built here with a GI Bill loan in 1948 cost $9,800, the lot $900. Bird Rock itself stands close offshore, frosted with guano. Because of wave erosion, owners of oceanfront lots spray their cliffs with gunite, hoping to preserve their houses. Bird Rockers are scrappy. They claim the best climate in La Jolla. Every June, when dismal offshore marine layers cloud most beaches until afternoon, Bird Rock is sunny.

Some who saw Pacific Beach in 1917 were thinking about ranchitas and citrus groves. But water has always been a problem: only seven to nine inches of rain fall in San Diego coastal areas during a good year, and almost none at all from April to December. Aqueducts built in the first half of the 20th century provide San Diego with water from the Colorado River, more than 200 miles away, and from northern California rivers, even more distant. Pacific Beach has no citrus groves now, but remains a middle-class beach town, a wondrous, yeasty blend of Midwest propriety and California bohemia.

For several generations, it seemed irresistible to some town developers to intrude on beautiful beaches with man-made structures. At Pacific Beach, Crystal Pier is a period piece that evokes images of the obsessed early migrants who flocked to Southern California and marched straight into the surf. This pier has its own motel over the crashing waves, and I'm part of a generation that thought taking a room at the Crystal Pier Motel was next-best to satanical. These days it's called Crystal Pier Motor Hotel, and some guests park on the pier. Hardly anyone goes there to avoid being seen.

(opposite) Like a glossy strip of oldtime ribbon candy, the Mission Beach roller coaster has survived to be reborn as a historic site. South from La Jolla the beach towns untold: Pacific Beach, then Mission, a beach in the Atlantic style: wide, gradual, graceful – and flat. The coaster, built in 1925, was restored and reopened to use in 1990. The amusement park was the bawdy center of San Diego beach life for two generations; its ballroom was the San Diego dance hall for the big band era. In the 1950s, inspired planners at San Diego's city hall turned to an ancient riverbed and marsh to create Mission Bay, a 4,800-acre aquatic park in the midst of the city. Dredging created islands, and then came beaches and inlets designed and zoned for diverse recreations: fishing, sailing, swimming, power-boating, model yachting, water skiing. Resort hotels followed, and the first Sea World amusement park. Mission Bay begins in the upper left of this picture.

Kelp beds in the Pacific off Point Loma are farmed by a fleet of seagoing threshers for agar, which is used to give some ice cream and beer its creamy feel, and to stabilize compounds that range from antacids to car polish. The harvesting vessels, which resemble giant lawn mowers, take the top four feet of kelp (Macrocystis Pyrifera) from beds leased from the state of California. Partly through the work of Scripps Institution of Oceanography, the beds are now recognized as important feeding grounds for many forms of aquatic life. Small boats pick their way carefully through these beds; long strands of kelp quickly foul propellers.

(below) When a leash law was passed by San Diego City Council in 1972, Dog Beach was exempted. At the northern edge of the fun-loving community of Ocean Beach, beside the San Diego River flood channel, Dog Beach is a place where dogs may go down to the sea without leashes. Their owners are, however, expected to clean up behind them. That fact surprised many in a crowd of 400 citizens who gathered one spring night in 1989, complaining to Ocean Beach Town Council of unsanitary conditions at Dog Beach. Dog owners promised finally that barrels, signs, scoops and peer pressure could solve the problem. Dog Beach retains its exemption.

(opposite) A treacherous sea has scalloped the shoreline at Sunset Cliffs and, beyond, Ocean Beach. Parking areas above the surf afford easy access, and unsuspecting inlanders are sometimes swept off these cliffs and drowned. At the top of the photograph are the wide blue expanses of Mission Bay, a mecca visited by city planners from around the world. Because of its shallowness, Mission Bay was known to early explorers as False Bay. When San Diego city planners began to study the bay in the 1950s, its tidal marshes held little charm. But its dredging provided a flood channel for the San Diego River, whose shifting course had created both Mission Bay and San Diego Bay. Some areas remain to be improved, but Mission Bay is one of the notable open spaces that give San Diego a sense of airiness.

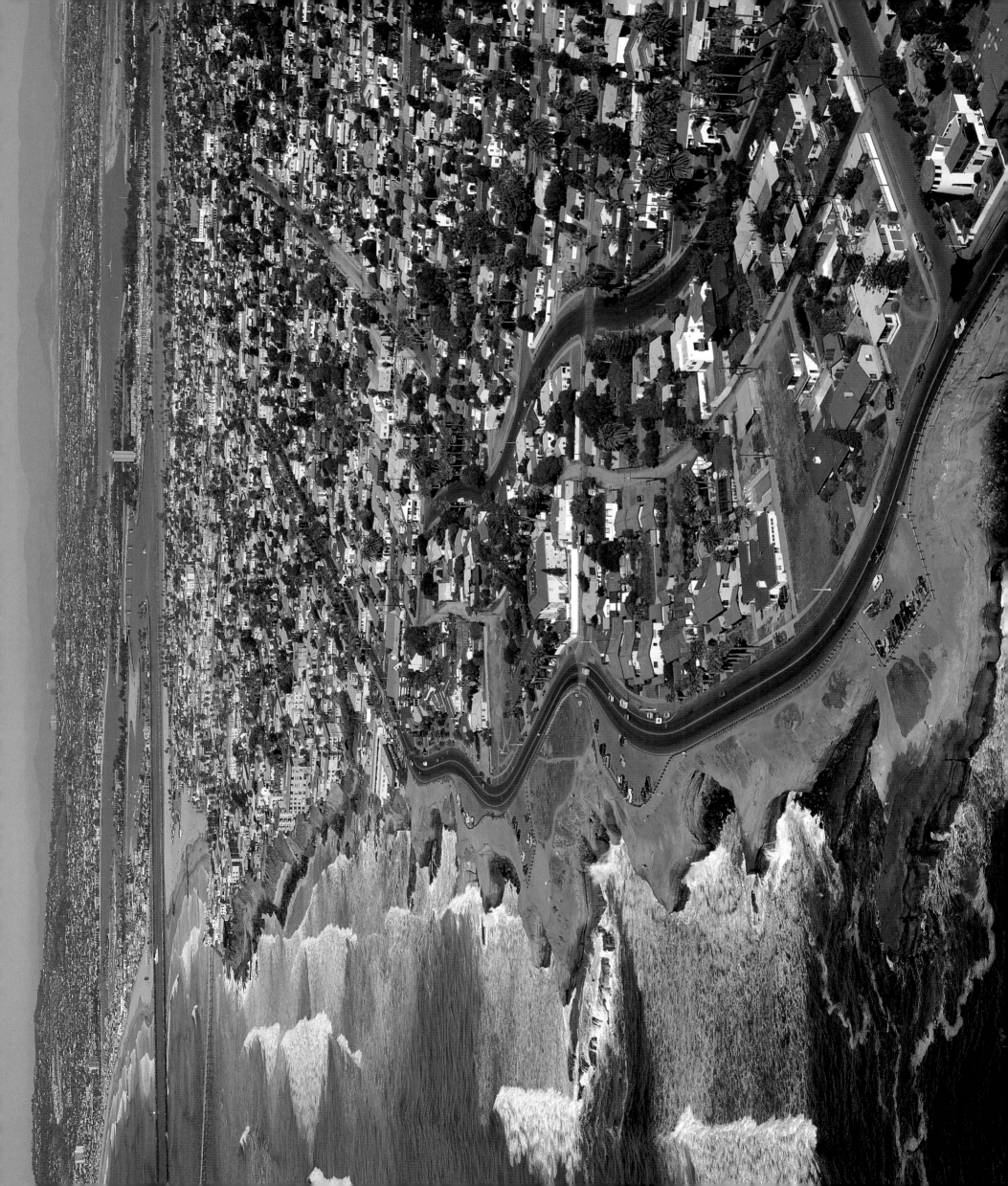

The compelling attraction at Cabrillo National Monument is the inland view, across San Diego Harbor, down the coast to Mexico and north toward Los Angeles. From here San Diego Harbor, twelve miles long, appears boot-shaped, its toes tucked into the sea. The monument is San Diego County's only outpost of the National Park System. For years it was a tenet of local pride that more visitors seek out Cabrillo National Monument than the Statue of Liberty. A statue honors the Portuguese explorer Juan Rodri'guez Cabrillo, the Columbus of California, who sailed into the harbor in 1542. He was the first European on the scene. The statue, donated by Portugal in 1939 to the San Francisco World's Fair, arrived too late, and was eventually erected here. The centerpiece of this enclave is the original Point Loma lighthouse, which served from 1855 until 1891, when the newer lighthouse (right), still in use, rose near water's edge. The house once occupied by the lighthouse keeper serves as quarters for the local commanding officer of the Coast Guard. In midwinter, California gray whales, migrating between the Bering Sea and Baja California, swim close past Point Loma.

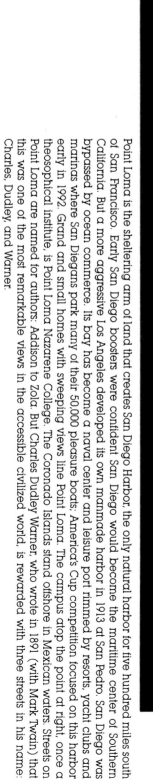

Point Loma is the sheltering arm of land that creates San Diego Harbor, the only natural harbor for five hundred miles south of San Francisco. Early San Diego boosters were confident San Diego would become the maritime center of Southern California. But a more aggressive Los Angeles developed its own manmade harbor in 1913 at San Pedro. San Diego was bypassed by ocean commerce. Its bay has become a naval center and leisure port rimmed by resorts, yacht clubs and marinas where San Diegans park many of their 50,000 pleasure boats; America's Cup competition focused on this harbor early in 1992. Grand and small homes with sweeping views line Point Loma. The campus atop the point at right, once a theosophical institute, is Point Loma Nazarene College. The Coronado Islands stand offshore in Mexican waters. Streets on Point Loma are named for authors: Addison to Zola. But Charles Dudley Warner, who wrote in 1891 (with Mark Twain) that this was one of the most remarkable views in the accessible civilized world, is rewarded with three streets in his name: Charles, Dudley, and Warner.

Hotel del Coronado opened in 1888, a fanciful Victorian resort built largely by Chinese laborers along a glorious wide beach. San Diego was in the midst of a brief land boom that brought development of the townsite around the hotel, snug between San Diego Harbor and the sea. The town of Coronado retains its own island-like identity today, an enclave of residential streets lined by big trees and an all-American amalgam of architectural styles, the dream houses of Navy and civilian migrants from every state of America. The hotel has become an important resort, but is still the center of a community that glorifies the hotel's history. Twelve United States presidents have slept here. State dinners have been held for presidents of the United States and Mexico. Wallis

Simpson, then a naval officer's wife, may or may not have met her future husband, the Duke of Windsor, when he dined here in 1920. But there's no doubt that Marilyn Monroe and Jack Lemmon wrote their footnotes in hotel history when "Some Like it Hot" was filmed here in 1958. Just south of the hotel along the sandspit known as Silver Strand, ten condo towers were built beside the beach in the 1970s. With that, Coronado residents mustered the clout to halt high-rise development. It's much the largest beachfront high-rise community in San Diego County, where rapid in-migration has made runaway growth the major political issue.

South of Coronado past Silver Strand State Beach, close to the top of the boot-shaped harbor and to Mexico, a high circular fence shields the tiny base called Naval Radio Facilities. In the years around World War II, tall antennas here transmitted urgent secret messages to ships and stations across the Pacific. More powerful and reliable communications systems have relegated the station to a lesser role. In the Pacific nearby, Navy frogmen undergo underwater training.

Seacoast Drive is the southernmost street of Imperial Beach, the southwesternmost town in the continental United States. On one side its residents hear the grinding crash of heavy breakers; on the other, the cries of gulls and geese along the Tijuana Slough National Wildlife Refuge. But no one mistakes the slough for the shores of La Jolla or Mission Bay. The estuary receives raw sewage down the Tijuana River, a putrid stream that snakes along the border. East of the slough is Imperial Beach Naval Auxiliary Landing Field, one of a network of ancillary fields maintained in support of the major naval air facilities at North Island and Miramar. Vehicles confiscated by federal narcotics officers are stored at the base until auctioned.

The Tijuana River bed crosses from Mexico into the United States about four miles inland from the sea. Along its final course in 1941 there were a few scattered farms on the American side. The river course was largely unchanged in 1990, and so were the farms. What had changed was foot traffic. On a typical night Border Patrolmen detain 600 to 800 illegal aliens, mostly Mexican laborers. Over this delta the patrols move on motor bikes, in steel-screened jeeps called war wagons, and in helicopters with searchlights. San Ysidro is the center of a surreal border zone that extends from the sands of Imperial

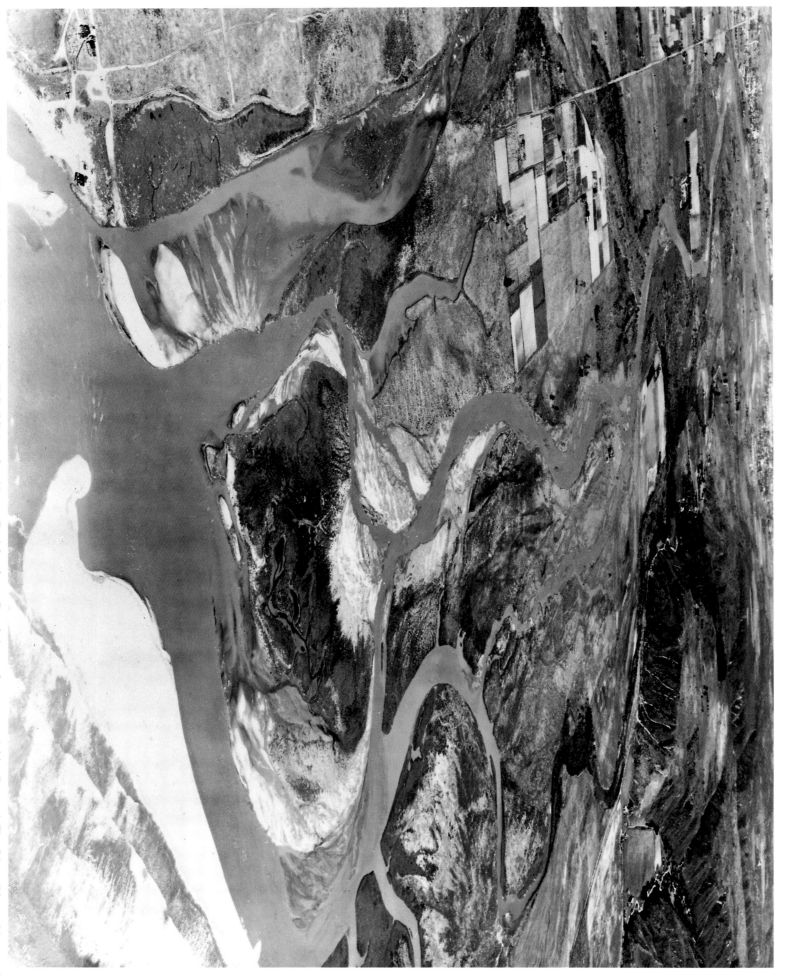

Beach to scrub canyons eight miles east. The 24 northbound lanes of vehicular traffic and the pedestrian gate at San Ysidro compose the busiest border crossing in the world, with close to 40 million persons passing through each year. The border between the United States and Mexico is 1,950 miles long, but as many as one-third of illegal aliens — a number rising at an estimated rate of 450,000 a year — cross in the San Diego sector, from the largest Mexican city along the border to the largest American city along the border. So far nothing has slowed the migration of Mexico's most desperate millions.

SAN DIEGO BAY

The casual neighboring of military and civilian in San Diego attests to an uncommonly respectful accord. Sailboats anchor in Glorietta Bay at Coronado just off the Naval Amphibious Base, where frogmen practice their dives off the public beaches of Silver Strand. Usually about 140,000 military people are on active duty in San Diego; about 40,000 have retired in the city. They receive close to four billion dollars a year in pay and retirement benefits.

(opposite) A century ago the California dream meant a house in the sunshine on a lot big enough for a few orange trees. By the 1950s it was the bungalow with a fenced patio in the back, and maybe, someday, a swimming pool. Now the dream is more exotic. Coronado Cays, built on a former dumpsite up-harbor from the town of Coronado, advances the premise that a Californian needs his own boat dock. Those who don't are just a stroll from Silver Strand State Beach. At Coronado Cays, most street names seem to have migrated, just like the residents. The yacht club is on Grand Caribe Isle. Your home may be on Mardi Gras Road or Antigua Court or Bahama Bend.

In the southern face of Point Loma, above San Diego Harbor and just over three miles from the downtown skyline, these bunkers hold unspecified submarine weapons and warheads. During World War II, these same hillsides held less sophisticated weapons: coastal artillery batteries. To the right, the Navy is building its most advanced attack-submarine school to train crews of the Seawolf-class submarines, joining the fleet in 1992 or 1993.

(opposite) Beyond the resort hotels, the marinas and the yacht clubs, some San Diego shores are off-limits. This is one of the Navy's controversial training projects: dolphin and sea lion pens at the Naval Ocean Systems Center. In 1962 the Navy began training sea mammals, including porpoises and whales, to exploit the creatures' unique sonar capabilities and their uncanny ability to learn. They were first used to retrieve practice torpedoes and act as underwater security guards. In 1988, the Navy reported a roster of 115 mammals, including about three dozen dolphins. Most are in San Diego, although there are periodic reports of dolphins in action. Dolphins were used in the Persian Gulf to search for mines but not, the Navy insists, to detonate them.

(*opposite*) The Naval Submarine Base, in the lee of Point Loma, is the Navy's largest attack submarine base and the primary training center for submarine crews. About fifteen submarines are usually assigned to this base, all of them nuclear-powered. They are of three classes: Permit, Sturgeon, and Los Angeles, with crews of as many as fifteen officers and 115 enlisted men. The base is on the site of a nineteenth-century Army coast defense fort. You can spot at least four submarines in this picture: one beside each of the two submarine tenders, and one in each of the dry docks. Then there's the little white sugar cube floating in the center: a three-story mobile berthing barge, affording temporary office space for transient crews.

Bob Cameron didn't tell the Navy he was doing portraits of nuclear submarines from Alan Kappmeier's helicopter, but there's no security breach here: a Sturgeon-class sub snugged up against a degaussing pier. In this process, a vessel is demag-netized for protection against magnetic mines. An electric current is passed along or around the vessel to neutralize the surrounding magnetic field. As at some of San Diego's other military facilities, there are surprising settings of timeless beauty within this base.

When New York editors visit San Diego in midwinter I take them to lunch at the San Diego Yacht Club. Even in January, we usually sit on the deck, an umbrella shielding us from the Southern California sun, and gaze out at this jungle of yachts, guessing how many tens of millions of floating dollars are in view. The scene bolsters the direst prejudices of Easterners who believe nothing of intellectual consequence could occur in such a setting. But of course the club's skippers include men and women who work at the vortex of a high-tech city. Their trophies include the America's Cup, won back from Australia for San Diego by that rascally skipper, Dennis Conner, after the Cup had spent generations on its pedestal at the New York Yacht Club.

The Southwestern Yacht Club has a wholesome reputation in San Diego as a family club; it's easier to join than the old-line San Diego Yacht Club. It's just a short tack southwest of the larger club, across an inlet from Shelter Island and in the lee of an upscale residential slope of Point Loma. Commercial marinas along the harbor accommodate most of the pleasure boats. Many of them have been made possible by dredging and landfilling that created two long hooks of land in the harbor, called Harbor Island and Shelter Island.

(opposite) Shelter Island was the idea, in the 1960s, of a port director named John Bate. He watched Navy dredges pile sand on barges as they kept harbor channels open for warships by dumping the spoil at sea. Then he studied San Diegans as they searched for places to keep their boats. He decided the fill from the barges could build a couple of nice islands in the harbor, one beside Point Loma, the other just across from San Diego International Airport. There were no environmental impact reports in those days. A few precious miles were added to the San Diego waterfront. If there's a hotter investment in San Diego than a beachfront house, it's a commercial marina. These tennis courts are part of the Kona Kai Club. The first phalanx of boats marks Silvergate Yacht Club. The pleasures of merer mortals aren't ignored. Picnic grounds, a fishing pier and boat launches are part of the public facilities along the harbor shore of Shelter Island.

Like Coronado, North Island isn't quite an island. But it juts out in the harbor like San Diego's front porch, doing what it's done since about the time the Wright Brothers flew: servicing military aviation. North Island was Army in World War I, but Navy ever since. My Navy orders in 1944 were to North Island Naval Air Station. A train porter pointed toward the harbor and advised me to take a passenger ferry called the Nickel Snatcher. From the red-tiled building with the tower, where I picked up my orders that day, naval aviators and aircraft carriers are directed around half the world, from the Arctic to the Antarctic and from California west across the Pacific and Indian oceans to the Persian Gulf. The base is temporary home to as many as 18,000 military personnel.

58

Some of the Navy's largest aircraft carriers are home-ported at North Island Naval Air Station, and become an imposing part of the harbor view. The carrier with the number 64 at its bow is the Constellation. Like its sister ships, it is a waterborne community of 5,000 men and a few pioneering women who patrol waters halfway around the world, as far as the east coast of Africa. (The command at Norfolk is responsible for the other half.) One night aboard the carrier Ranger, 60 miles southwest of San Diego, I watched young Navy pilots practice landings. Their 24-ton F-14 Tomcats slammed down on the deck at full power, about 140 to 150 miles an hour. They have split-second chances for their hooks to engage arresting cables; if they are three or four feet high, they must fly around again. On that night a troubled pilot tried repeatedly to land and, running out of fuel, was ordered back to shore, likely to lose his treasured wings.

Navy helicopters line this parking ramp at North Island Naval Air Station, served by mechanics who work out of the two large hangars. Attack helicopters, including these Navy H-46s, are used to drop torpedos or recover them in anti-submarine warfare. The city of Coronado is in the background, linked to downtown San Diego by the bridge at left. South of Coronado, the narrow Silver Strand leads toward the distant hills of Mexico's Baja California.

The real name of San Diego International Airport is Lindbergh Field; in one of its central mazes is a bust of Charles Lindbergh, who ordered his *Spirit of St. Louis* from the nearby Ryan Airlines shop early in 1927. On May 10 he took off from North Island in the *Spirit* to fly eastward and make aviation history: the first non-stop flight across the Atlantic, a solo from New York to Paris on May 20-21, taking 33 hours and 29 minutes. No event since the end of World War I had so absorbed the world. Now San Diegans are schizophrenic about the location of the airport that bears Lindbergh's name. It is beside the central harbor, and the glide path of landing jets seems perilously close to tall buildings. Their take-offs rattle dishes in Point Loma homes. But for hundreds of thousands of San Diegans, the airport seems conveniently close. For forty years, and through a score of consultants' studies, all talk of relocating the airport has led to nothing.

Lindbergh Field could be enlarged and stay put indefinitely, some San Diegans argue, if the United States Marine Corps would kindly move its adjacent Recruit Depot north to suburban Camp Pendleton. No way, the generals say; this site has been hallowed by Marines since 1921. All male recruits enlisted west of the Mississippi come here for twelve weeks of training. Their arduous drills and eventually their graduation ceremonies occur on this 2,200-foot-long parade ground, known as The Grinder. About a million marines have trained here since 1923, currently at the rate of about 23,000 a year. Pride and tradition lie deep. Bertram Goodhue, the architect involved with San Diego's exposition in 1915-16, designed Senior Officers' Quarters in the style he called Spanish Colonial Revival. The base has 21 buildings listed in the National Register of Historic Places.

Major cruise ships schedule occasional stops at San Diego, but the city's old cul-de-sac syndrome is still at work: Just 100 miles north is Los Angeles Harbor, closer to Disneyland and Hollywood, and to more direct jet connections. So Los Angeles is usually the embarkation and disembarkation port of choice. Smaller ships such as the Southward make regular runs out of San Diego, most often for Mexican west coast ports.

(opposite) Harbor Island was the second of John Bate's new almost-islands, and marinas for pleasure boats have not been overlooked. But Harbor Island is adjacent to the airport, and hotel builders have vied for sites zoned for lodging. Sheraton has two large hotels on Harbor Island, and Stouffer has been awarded the final available site.

64

Along San Diego's Embarcadero, tuna clippers and purse seiners tied bow to stern in the decades before the tuna industry moved largely offshore. Now visitors are drawn instead to the ships of the Maritime Museum. The three-masted Star of India is the oldest iron sailing ship afloat – and the oldest ship of any type still sailing. She was launched at Ramsey in the Isle of Man in 1863, five days before Lincoln delivered his Gettysburg Address. The Star sailed in the emigrant traffic from Britain to Australia and New Zealand between 1871 and 1897. Just beyond her floats the Berkeley, the second propeller-driven ferryboat on the Pacific Coast, which helped evacuate refugees from the San Francisco earthquake and fire in 1906. The red-tiled building near the Berkeley is a San Diego landmark: the County Administration Center, built in 1935 by the Works Progress Administration. On the right, the county building and Star of India at night.

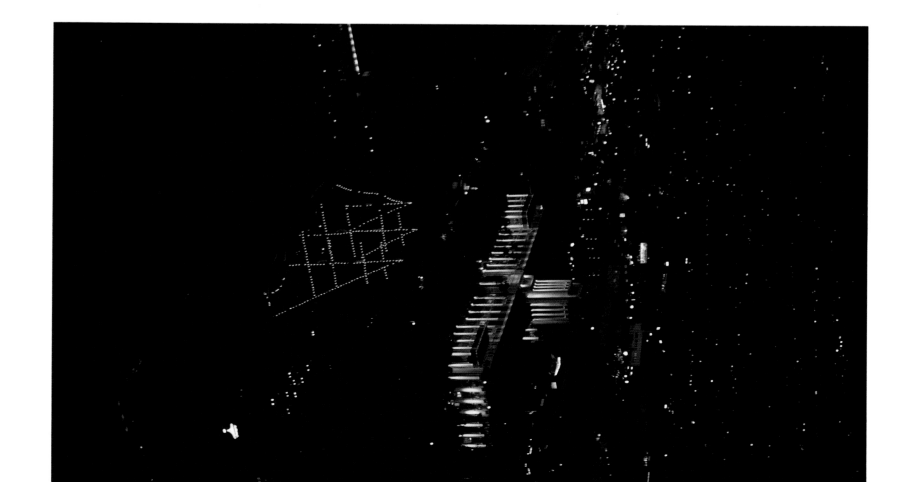

San Diego's Unified Port District is that ultimate rarity: a governmental agency with more money than it needs. It owns the tidelands along San Diego Harbor, including the airport, and takes leasehold royalties from sales at harbor-front restaurants, hotels, clubs and marinas. Much of its largesse has gone to shoreline enhancement and to fund a San Diego convention center completed in 1990. This small fishing-boat basin, called Tuna Harbor, caters largely to overnight commercial fishermen.

Seaport Village is a fanciful collection of tile-roofed shops and restaurants. A wide pedestrian promenade begins here and winds on past the site of a scheduled Hyatt Regency Hotel, yet another marina (astronaut Wally Schirra keeps his boat here), and the Marriott Hotel to the Convention Center. If San Diego needed a symbolic main street, this promenade would serve. It affords sweeping harbor views and a rich sampling of the amenities that represent the San Diego style.

(opposite) Although there's scant cargo traffic in San Diego Harbor, shipyards vie for waterfront space beside hotels and marinas. This towering crane at Campbell Shipyard was large enough to hoist Michael Fay's big New Zealand yacht in his abortive America's Cup challenge of 1988. That's the Marriott marina just beyond, enclosed by the landscaped paths of Embarcadero Marina Park. The low, white-roofed structure at the left of the crane is a Chart House restaurant. It occupies the former San Diego Rowing Club house. For years, Rowing Club members leaped from here into the bay each New Year's Day for a ritual swim, a chilling tradition they continue at a new club site.

San Diegans paid cash for this convention center, completed in 1990; it was a $165,000,000 gift from the royalties-rich Port Authority. Architect Arthur Erickson, celebrating the bayside site, thought nautical: arched skylights and teflon-coated canvas sails suggest some hybrid seagoing vessel. At the time of its completion it was the largest meeting and exhibit hall on the West Coast. It also was San Diego's most expensive locally-funded public works project, its largest public building, and a popular symbol of urban renewal. The lower of its two basement garages extends below the mean tide line and requires perpetual pumping. San Diego's snappy red trolleys link the convention center with an expanding light rail route.

(opposite) The almost-twin mirrored towers of the San Diego Marriott reflect the glitter of San Diego bay and sun and a rapidly improving downtown scene. The first building, at right, was designed as a parabola. Complexities of construction and of the resultant floor-plan led to a square-ended design for the second tower. The hotel is next-door to San Diego's new convention center. Directly across the bay is Coronado.

Purse seiners tied up at the Port's Tenth Avenue Terminal are highlighted by a setting sun, bringing a glow to the yellow floats that sustain their fishing nets. A short-haul fishing boat returns from offshore waters to Tuna Harbor. At National Steel and Shipbuilding, right, the *Exxon Valdez* prepares for drydock repairs to its hull, torn when the tanker ran aground in Prince William Sound near Valdez, Alaska, in 1989, an accident that loosed a flood of oil and led to an environmental revolt. A rock almost the size of a Volkswagen Bug was removed from the hull. San Diegans suggested it be displayed at bayside as public art to parody a long agony of Port Commission indecision in commissioning public art. But Exxon spokespeople claimed ownership of the rock, and did not appear amused at the suggestion. The tanker emerged from drydock, its hull restored and its name changed to the *Exxon Mediterranean*. Superstitious sailors remained skeptical. *Mediterranean*, a 13-letter word, is considered an unlucky name.

The splendid Reuben E. Lee, docked at the tip of Harbor Island, is the kind of showboat restaurant to which San Diegans take visiting relatives. It's five minutes from Lindbergh Field and downtown. Although the structure rocks gently with tidal changes, it was built at the site as a restaurant atop a barge that is permanently docked. It serves up to 600 diners, and is favored for wedding receptions. An identical sister restaurant is in Newport Beach.

(opposite) San Diego's favorite party boats are the two riverboat sternwheelers of Mission Bay, docked here beside the Bahia Hotel. The smaller boat, on the far side of the pier, is the Bahia Belle; the larger, closer to the camera, is the newer William D. Evans. It's all short skirts, ruffles and garters, jazz and Dixieland, as the boats spiral around the inlets and under the bridges of Mission Bay, calling at the Bahia's sister hotel, the Catamaran.

There are a dozen major Navy and Marine Corps facilities in San Diego County, but the dominant ship base is the Naval Station, an almost self-sustaining city that flanks two miles of harborfront and docks close to a hundred warships. Its stores, courthouse, brig, service stations, clubs, restaurants, housing office and child care centers are familiar to men and women throughout the Pacific fleet. The view at left is to the southeast.

(opposite) One of San Diego's best waterfront views belongs to 250 Coast Guard men and women at their snug air station beside San Diego Harbor. With three mid-range Falcon jets and four Dauphin helicopters, they fly missions in air and sea emergencies, sometimes as distant as 700 miles and more from base. Now a major mission is drug interdiction. The station was founded in 1934 to combat smugglers crossing the border from Mexico. In later years when a major tuna fleet was based in San Diego Harbor, these fliers were the fishermen's rescue link. They have flown many mercy missions off the long Mexican coast of Baja California, leaving rescue assignments with San Diego's big pleasure boat fleet largely to Coast Guard surface vessels. The Coast Guard fliers' own traffic signal halts cars along Harbor Drive so they can taxi aircraft to and from Lindbergh Field runways.

In watery nooks of San Diego Harbor, eccentric houseboaters pose a challenge to Harbor Police and to local codes; jurisdiction of San Diego Harbor is shared through the Unified Port District by the contiguous cities of San Diego, Coronado, Imperial Beach, Chula Vista, and National City. One vessel that's been the object of scrutiny by both city building inspectors and the Coast Guard is the party barge Excalibur, known as The Castle. It was built from four surplus fiberglass Navy landing craft to accommodate up to 300 people, and is anchored in shallow water off Chula Vista's J Street Pier. At last report, The Castle was in decline as a furniture storehouse.

(opposite) Salt has been made beside the shallows of San Diego Harbor since the mid-19th century. Today about 1,200 acres are used by Western Salt Co. to produce about 75,000 tons a year through evaporation. The natural sloping of the bay and gravity are used to trap and transfer seawater, assisted by electric pumps. About 30 ponds are separated by levees, and water moves through three stages for 18 to 24 months until it is mined as solid salt. A gallon of water yields about three ounces of salt, which takes its place in a "salt mountain" that is a landmark just west of Interstate 5 at Chula Vista. This salt isn't pure enough for table use; it's used to treat water, tan hides, make dye, and pickle food.

DOWNTOWN

The campus of San Diego City College is well-placed between a redeveloping downtown and Balboa Park. With 14,000 students, it is considered the flagship of the community college system in San Diego. In addition, there are two northside campuses, Mesa and Miramar, and a complex in Southeast San Diego. City College was the third junior college established in California after the state legislature, in 1907, authorized two-year higher education institutions as an adjunct to high school public education. In its role of vocational education, the college works with the Navy to provide courses in quality control for defense contractors, in computer design and in court reporting.

(opposite) The University of San Diego is the city's picture-book campus: gleaming white buildings in the 16th-century plateresque style of the Spanish Renaissance. Many of them have richly landscaped inner courtyards that offer a serenity rarely found on university campuses. The campus occupies 180 acres atop a mesa that overlooks Mission Bay and Old Town San Diego State Historic Park, where California began. The centerpiece is the blue-domed Immaculata Church. The university director of design, a post rare among colleges, is Therese Whitcomb, an art professor who was in the first graduating class of its College for Women. She is quick to contrast campus style with the baroque buildings of Balboa Park, associated with a later Spanish era. Chartered in 1949, University of San Diego is an independent Catholic institution with four-year undergraduate programs and graduate programs that include a distinguished law school. There are about 6,000 students.

Between the two world wars, San Diego Naval Station's mothball fleet was the Navy's attic. It contained as many as 223 retired war vessels, including these 40 destroyers. Even after the end of World War II, there were musty, creaky submarines dating back to the 1920s, and a horde of military weaponry that was eventually scrapped to help make more sophisticated tools of war. Today the cobwebs are all gone. With its network of piers and docks, the Naval Station is the primary military facility in San Diego for major warships, usually about 100. It vies intermittently with Norfolk for rank as host to the largest concentration of warships in the world.

When helicopter pilot Alan Kappmeier took Bob Cameron up to about 3,000 feet, downtown San Diego looked like this (left), with Balboa Park the green enclave at left, and the coastal mountains rising out beyond East San Diego, La Mesa, El Cajon, Lakeside and Santee. That's Tuna Harbor in the foreground. Back closer to earth, the camera picks up overhead views of several blocks of low-rise housing communities, Park Row and Marina Park, that sparked the beginning of downtown redevelopment about 1980. The tall beige building is a federal prison; towering over it at far right is the Meridian, a condominium tower that for the first time brought multi-million-dollar apartments to downtown.

84

The years from 1769 to 1822 made up the Spanish period in San Diego, then a dusty pueblo of mud and thatch huts and a single church. The neighborhood is now Old Town San Diego State Historic Park, close to the intersection of two interstate freeways, north-south 5 and east-west 8. Most of the landmarks of the park are restored from the Mexican Period (1822-1848). Most notable are Casa de Estudillo, largest of the adobes, once occupied by the Spanish commander of the presidio; and Casa de Bandini, once Old Town's social center, in use now as a Mexican restaurant. Old Town Plaza is the grassy block at the center of the park's inner walking area. In the county-operated Heritage Park (right), just south of Old Town Park, fine Victorian houses, notably the Sherman-Gilbert, have been brought in from other San Diego neighborhoods and restored.

Like those of many cities, San Diego's street cars disappeared soon after World War II in a well-orchestrated lobbying effort to put Americans in their cars and on freeways. With freeways moving close to capacity, San Diegans return to the rails in one of the nation's most successful restorations of trolley service. Outside Metropolitan Transit Development Board headquarters downtown, San Diego's bright red trolleys find parking room. The first and most profitable run is to Tijuana, 12 miles from downtown San Diego. A newer route to the east is clicking away, and others are on the way. Mayor Maureen O'Connor brags that ticket sales pay almost 90 percent of the system's operating costs.

In 1985 four seedy downtown blocks became a fanciful shopping village called Horton Plaza. It was a home-town production for Ernie Hahn, a highly successful shopping center developer who had retired in Rancho Santa Fe and begun to devote his time to civic volunteerism. Jon Jerde, who had designed the Los Angeles Olympic Games, was the architect, and he seemed to baffle critics. Horton Plaza is a theatrical hodgepodge of Venetian and Spanish and Southwest themes, cast in frivolous shapes and rebellious colors, and at unexpected angles. Critics slowly came to accept it as a new generation of playful design intended to blur the worlds of shopping and entertainment. Horton Plaza has been a financial success; more, it has been a major factor in bringing San Diegans back downtown.

In 1911 the U.S. Grant Hotel (lower center) had just been dedicated. Glenn Curtis was establishing a flying school at North Island, the barren area just beneath Point Loma, on the horizon at top. There was a Mexican revolution in Baja California, and Tijuana was taken over by rebels. With a population of only 40,000, San Diego broke ground in Balboa Park for the Panama-California Exposition. The photograph at right was taken in 1990 from almost the same point in the air as the 1911 photograph. The Grant Hotel, recently restored, is still there, across Broadway from Horton Plaza. It's hard to find anything else unchanged except the fountain in the plaza.

From near the same point as the pictures on two preceding pages, the cameras here are turned to face northeast across San Diego and its suburban cities toward the coastal mountains. The year, at left, is 1915, when the Panama-California Exposition opened, bringing money to a city that was nearly broke. It also created, in Balboa Park, a community of neo-Spanish Colonial buildings, some of which remain. The Boston architect Bertram Goodhue was the prime mover, with the local Irving J. Gill as his assistant. The graceful arches of Cabrillo Bridge, still in use, reflect the simple California style of Gill; Goodhue's mark was a baroque amalgam drawn from Spanish and Mexican colonial styles, akin to the Churrigueresque tradition of Salamanca. In the 1990 photograph at right, bridge and California Tower remain. The most prominent newer park structure is the circular Ford Building, from the later exposition of 1935.

To find some link between the San Diego of World War I and the 1990s, look for the twin mission towers of the Santa Fe Station at left-center in the earlier photograph, and at lower center in the newer one. About eight blocks up Broadway, in the older picture, you'll find the Grant Hotel. It's still there in the 1990s, but dwarfed by newer office towers.

This high view from above San Diego Harbor in 1935 is a primer for students of shifting shorelines. In 1911, the California Legislature had granted some cities control of their tidelands. San Diego already had more than twenty miles of harborfront, and this became an almost incalculable urban wealth. After years of dredging and reshaping, the downtown harborfront is drastically revised, especially in the neighborhood of Lindbergh Field.

96

In 1936 Broadway was indisputably San Diego's main street, and it led down to the waterfront and Broadway Pier. On one side was a Navy citadel; headquarters of the old Eleventh Naval District. On the other was Lane Field, home of the Pacific Coast League Padres. Time hasn't improved this neighborhood. Baseball has moved out to San Diego Jack Murphy Stadium in Mission Valley, and cars now park where San Diego-born Theodore Samuel Williams made his baseball debut in 1936. Ted Williams played with little

distinction here for two years before going up to the Boston Red Sox in 1939 on his way to the National Baseball Hall of Fame. Even after he became a legendary hitter, the last player to bat over .400, his mother carried on at her chosen work in San Diego, ringing a bell beside a Salvation Army kettle. Though he is a baseball immortal, Williams' name, curiously, has not yet been awarded to any public street or facility in his sports-wild home town.

ENVIRONS

In 1769 a 55-year-old Franciscan mission priest, Junípero Serra, marched 350 miles up through Mexican desert to San Diego Harbor. As accompanying Spanish soldiers set up a presidio, he dedicated a small brushwood hut as the first California mission. The site is known today as Presidio Park, above Old Town Plaza. Serra's mission is commonly hailed as the start of the white man's California. In 1774 the mission, plagued by hostile Indians and short of water, was rebuilt seven miles east in Mission Valley. In its heyday, the mission controlled 50,000 acres and owned thousands of sheep, cattle, and horses. It has been charmingly restored as a parish church and visitor attraction.

(opposite) Mission San Luis Rey de Francia, about three miles inland from Oceanside, was founded in 1798, the 18th in the California chain of 21 missions. By 1832 its priests claimed the baptism of more than six thousand Indians. Today, handsomely restored and serving the Franciscan order, it has become a major social resource of the North County region. Its adult education classes range from Joyce to Jung. Social workers are on 24-hour call. Children with behavioral problems air them out at summer day camp. Several masses are said each day in Spanish, serving a large Hispanic migrant community.

Scripps Clinic and Research Foundation moved from downtown La Jolla in 1976 to Torrey Pines Mesa, overlooking the sea. Here it joined Salk Institute and the University of California in an explosion of bioscience research that marked the beginnings of modern San Diego. Scripps has since grown into the largest private biomedical research institute in the world. It receives more research funds from the National Institutes of Health than any other private organization.

(opposite) Serra Museum stands atop Presidio Hill overlooking Old Town and Interstate 8, which winds eastward through Mission Valley. A monument to mission architecture, it was built in 1929. Its funding patron was one of San Diego's early merchant princes, George Marston, best remembered for his passion in building parks. Serra Museum houses one of the museums of the San Diego Historical Society. Its research library is public.

San Diego has multiple downtowns, population hubs, and central intersections. One is this crossing of two major freeways in Mission Valley. Interstate 8, which unwinds eastward toward mountains, desert, and Arizona; and State 163, which leads from the traditional downtown through Balboa Park and northward through a corridor of rapid residential growth. Delivery trucks of The San Diego Union-Tribune roll out from the newspaper headquarters at the center of this photograph; in the background is Fashion Valley, San Diego's busiest shopping mall. Above it are the apartment complexes of North Rim. A generation or two ago, much of this valley was dairyland.

Soon after the University of California announced plans for a major campus in San Diego in 1962, its medical school took over the old County Hospital as the site of a new teaching center. Since then its surgeons and staff have pioneered many procedures, including heart and lung transplants. Today the UCSD Medical Center operates in a dozen buildings and ranks high in hospital listings. Its infant care center serves San Diego and Imperial counties. The UCSD School of Medicine ranks fourth in the United States in amount of research funding; it supports work in aging, AIDS, cancer, genetics, ophthalmology, and Alzheimer's disease.

Miramar Naval Air Station is the Navy's top fighter base, home of the carrier pilots celebrated in the movie "Top Gun." It is surprisingly near the present geographic center of San Diego population: the hills of La Jolla are on the horizon. The station and its long runways were shut down in the years soon after World War II, and the Navy held discussions with the city of San Diego about selling the city the property. But in that small-town era it seemed too far to the north of the city and from need. So the Navy invested hundreds of millions of dollars and reopened Miramar. With city support, it purchased and zoned a broad buffer zone. Now, with Lindbergh Field overcrowded, San Diego politicians long for a second chance to acquire Miramar.

Regional shopping malls provide a very real sense of community in areas of San Diego County where chaparral hills have become instant suburbs. North County Fair, in southern Escondido, has become the third busiest mall in the county, serving new communities along the north-south Interstate 15 corridor. To its east, in the background, is San Pasqual Valley, site of a city agricultural preserve and the Zoo's Wild Animal Park.

In San Diego, red tile roofs may signal planned communities with neo-Spanish motifs. Rancho Bernardo, spanning Interstate 15 between San Diego and Escondido, is a planned community that has meticulously maintained its design integrity. In 1962, developers Harry Summers and Fritz Hawn chased grazing cattle off 5,400 rolling acres of the former Daley Ranch and began building a town that now has about 28,000 residents. The community gains diversity and balance from its industrial park, its golf and tennis facilities, and a distinguished resort, Rancho Bernardo Inn.

The *ne plus ultra* of horsey San Diego is Rancho Santa Fe, a covenanted community inland from Del Mar and Encinitas. Tall, pungent eucalyptus trees shade thousands of acres here because of one of local history's wonderful jokes. Early in the century, the Santa Fe railroad imported eucalyptus seedlings from Australia to grow on semi-desert hillsides here. The trees were to be used as railroad ties. But they were never harvested; spikes wouldn't hold in the brittle wood. The tree farm became a real estate venture. Soon after World War II it began to thrive. Bing Crosby and Howard Hughes had houses here. So do Robert Young, Victor Mature, Patti Page, and a continuing procession of corporate and professional celebrities who treasure its roomy, uncommercial privacy. Ronald

Reagan's brother Neil lives here, professing sympathy that the former president settled for retirement in Los Angeles' Bel Air. The retired astronaut Walter Schirra and his wife Jo planned their home here when he was a test pilot at Miramar. The lawn at the village center is the croquet court of the snug Inn at Rancho Santa Fe. Just beyond is the three-block Rancho Santa Fe downtown, including Mille Fleurs and Delicias restaurants. About 21,000 people lived in Rancho Santa Fe in 1990. Their median household income led all San Diego communities: about $60,000. But estates are changing hands and character. During 1989 and 1990, seventeen of the town's 1,600 dwellings were sold for $1 million or more but razed to make space for larger houses.

Spacious acreage distinguishes the great estates of San Diego. In Rancho Santa Fe, citrus and eucalyptus groves, lakes, and stables serve as privacy barriers on lots with a minimum size of one acre; a fairway-sized lawn becomes a modern sculpture garden. Homes within the inner covenant area, controlled through a homeowners' association, are most prized. It took hard salesmanship fifty years ago to dispose of lots, but Rancho Santa Fe now has international cachet among the wealthy. There's rarely any home on agents' lists under a million dollars. In La Jolla, below, residents of these homes on the west-facing slope of Mount Soledad enjoy the eighteen holes of La Jolla Country Club as a vast front-lawn above the Pacific.

Fairbanks Ranch emerged as an almost instant estate community in the 1980s, on land southwest of Rancho Santa Fe that had been owned by the film actor Douglas Fairbanks. In 1984 it hosted the Olympic Games equestrian events. Developer Ray Watt built future forests on scrubland as he planted thousands of trees. Horses and golf are the leisure attractions; Wayne Lukas trained many winning thoroughbreds here in the expansive stables of the late Gene Klein. The most renowned resident is Joan Kroc, widow of the man who developed the McDonald's chain and owned the San Diego Padres. Although homesites sell in the million-dollar range and finished homes for many millions, the median age of homeowners in an early Fairbanks Ranch survey was 42. The fourteen-acre estate, above, occupies ten homesites.

One of the ultimate luxuries in a neigh-borhood of million-dollar lots and of drought-rationed water is a polo ground like this one, owned by the Rancho Santa Fe Polo Club. Players and ponies some-times trailer in from Palm Springs and Santa Barbara for leisurely matches; some San Diego players stable their ponies in the barns at the edge of this field, in the San Dieguito River valley east of the Del Mar racetrack.

(opposite) Whispering Palms Golf Club lies between Rancho Santa Fe and Fair-banks Ranch and in the valley of the San Dieguito River. It is the center of a com-munity of about 600 residents. Golfers can play a different course each day of the week within five miles. Among them are courses at the Rancho Santa Fe Country Club, Rancho Santa Fe Farms, Fairbanks Country Club, Lomas Santa Fe, and Heritage.

113

(opposite) La Costa Country Club opened inland from Carlsbad in 1965, notorious for its Las Vegas-linked proprietors and its $57 million loan from a Teamsters pension fund. In 1975 Penthouse magazine portrayed La Costa as a mob hangout and was hit with a $522 million libel suit, settled quietly out of court ten years later. Through the years, La Costa's health spa has steadily gained world renown. When the resort was sold in 1987 to Sports Shinko Co., the price was $250 million. For that the Japanese operators received two 18-hole golf courses, 23 tennis courts, seven restaurants, and 482 guest rooms. The original owners, including film and TV producer Merv Adelson, then husband of television's Barbara Walters, had already split off their last 3,600 undeveloped acres to Daon Corporation of Canada for $110 million, the largest single land transaction prior to 1981 in San Diego history.

Most of the hundreds of thousands who have migrated to San Diego talk about being drawn by economic and leisure opportunity, climate, and escape. But when newspaper baron E. W. Scripps visited San Diego in 1890, he saw it as a busted boom town and bought a 400-acre ranch north of town because it was a place to hide. "3,000 miles from the people who bothered me about my newspaper." He called his ranch Miramar, or sea view. These days it's Scripps Ranch, one of San Diego's more gracious residential communities. Its Miramar Lake is a city reservoir. Its lakeside trail has become the leisure center of a community of about 12,000 residents.

Waterfalls are part of architectural walls at Wateridge Corporate Park, a 125-acre enclave near the junction of two northbound interstates, 5 and 805. Among tenants in 125 adjacent acres is Science Applications International Corp., a unique employee-owned, high-technology research and development company with annual sales of about $800 million, including the first airline security device capable of detecting plastic bombs.

(opposite) Flower growers were quick to exploit San Diego's benign climate. Their farms and greenhouses are increasingly squeezed by residential growth and water shortages. Still, the long growing season is enjoyed by growers in scattered tracts of the north San Diego coast near Encinitas and Carlsbad. On his 900-acre poinsettia farm, Paul Ecke produces 90 percent of the mother plants from which growers around the world produce the familiar potted flowers for the year-end holiday season. A daily flower auction is held in a huge co-op market at Carlsbad, the Floral Trade Center. Because of their prolific production, carnations became the official San Diego flower.

(*opposite*) San Diego's Golden Triangle seems to have just arrived, east of La Jolla in the corridor between freeways 5 and 805. A shopping mall called University Towne Center appeared out in the chaparral east of the University of California campus, and soon high-rises surrounded it. One is a Marriott hotel that carries the name of La Jolla, just one of countless outriders on a magic, though untranslatable name. Locals were skeptical that guests would find their way to the new hotel. But it had 90 percent occupancy in its first year, and was soon joined by other hotels. Critics of Golden Triangle insist it reminds them of adjacent Orange County, a very bad thing to say in San Diego County. But it was in Golden Triangle that the San Diego Chamber of Commerce opened its first branch office when it appeared that San Diego might be migrating northward without its official civic boosters.

Architect Michael Graves found a client in the developer Jack Naiman who encouraged him to do it his way – from severe, neo-classic exterior lines to Egyptian palm court and to hotel furnishings, from dresser to ashtray. The Aventine complex rises from a sea of new residences just east of La Jolla. It opened in 1990, to include a Hyatt Regency hotel, office building, and health club of Roman proportions. Communities of town houses and condos are covering the adjacent mesas. They are occupied predominantly by young singles and families involved in education, research and development, financial and real estate services, and the professions. The accelerated in-migration of such residents during the 1980s helped to give San Diego a promising distinction: Among residents of the nation's ten most populous cities, it has the highest percentage of college graduates.

Those San Diegans who oppose further population growth point toward scenes like this. In North City West, inland from Del Mar, hills are leveled for building pads in a community where 40,000 residents are expected by the end of the 1990s. The first earthmovers arrived in this 4,286-acre development in 1982 after years of political debate. Three years later, Del Mar phone books added the line, "Including North City West." There are plans for 14,000 houses and apartments, office buildings and light industry sites. Most of the neighborhood parks originally promised by developers have disappeared from the community plan. New San Diegans need houses. But as they settle in, many join the ranks of anti-growth.

(opposite) The deep green foliage of avocado groves has replaced the glitter of citrus orchards on many back-country hillsides. San Diego County is the nation's leading producer of avocados. Drip systems make it possible to irrigate trees on steep slopes. Farm laborers from south of the border clamber over the hills at harvest time. Scenes like this are common in rural communities of the foothills: from Escondido west and north to San Marcos, Vista, Fallbrook, Bonsall, Pauma Valley and Valley Center. Although flowers, nursery stock and indoor decorative plants make up about half of the San Diego agricultural base, avocados come next with a value of more than $100 million annually. With almost $800 million in agriculture production each year, San Diego ranks, surprisingly, among California's ten leading farm counties. But almost half of the dollar volume is in nursery and flower products.

Beneath a central green pyramid roof, the San Diego Design Center dominates an industrial plateau on Sorrento Mesa. Opened in 1989 at a cost of $33 million, it provides 100 showrooms aimed at matching rival centers to the north in attracting designers. The old cry of Los Angeles dominance is implicit when San Diego decorators talk of no longer having to drive their clients to another city to choose carpeting, fabric, and furnishings. Oldtime San Diegans call this the "kid glove syndrome," recalling that, for years, proper San Diego women had nowhere to send their kid gloves for cleaning but to Los Angeles.

The opening of the first college of the University of California at San Diego in 1964 marked the threshold of modern San Diego. The beginning faculty was studded with Nobel laureates and distinguished in the biological sciences; some academic stars were inherited from the much older Scripps Institution of Oceanography, which became part of the university campus. UCSD attracted eminent academicians and researchers to San Diego. Today it ranks among the top ten research universities in the nation, and stands fifth in the sum of federal funding for research. It is first among public universities in the percentage of undergraduates who go on to medical school and to earn doctoral degrees. It has been a catalyst in the growth of a major biosciences industry in San Diego. About 16,000 students attend UCSD's five undergraduate colleges and graduate schools on the campus just north of La Jolla. There are more than 14,000 staff and academic employees, making it the third largest employer in San Diego County.

Camp Pendleton Marine Corps Base is peacetime home to about 32,000 military men and women and 2,500 civilians. But it has an even stronger claim on the loyalty of San Diegans: Its 125,000 acres of open space, acquired from ranchers as World War II loomed, provide a 17-mile-long buffer along the county's north coast and 20 miles inland to the east. To environmentalists, it seems an irony that this training base for the military provides the county's purest ecological area. As home of the First Marine Division, Camp Pendleton has served as part of embarkation for marines going to duty in the Pacific and around the world since World War II. Its airstrip is the home of Marine Aircraft Group 39. The base seemed nearly vacated during the Persian Gulf war in early 1991.

(opposite) Space telescopes haven't made Palomar Mountain Observatory obsolete. The 200-inch Hale telescope, installed in 1948, still serves as an astronomers' workhorse atop Palomar Mountain, 6,000 feet high in the forests near San Diego County's north inland border. In Southern California, quick changes in altitude afford sudden climatic variations. This is high country where, in times of winter storms, coastal San Diego families go for a day of frolic in the snow. The observatory is owned and operated by the California Institute of Technology. Its research centers on how and when the first galaxies were formed. San Diegans have sought to preserve the clear bright skies above Palomar by converting street illumination in the city to low-glare sodium vapor lights.

124

For decades, much of the world knew little about San Diego except for its zoo. Within Balboa Park, at the traditional heart of the city, the zoo has exploited the San Diego climate. It has pioneered in open-air enclosures, free of bars, to house its vast animal population. Research at the zoo hospital evolved into the Center for Reproduction of Endangered Species, where scientists work to enhance the fertility of animals. With DNA fingerprinting and gene structure studies, they manage rare-animal mating to produce offspring, some of which are returned to native habitats. CRES helped to breed Przewalski's horses, which had disappeared from their habitat in the Gobi Desert: eleven horses have

been returned to northwest China. CRES also was involved in reintroducing the Arabian oryx in its native deserts of Oman, Jordan, Israel, and Saudi Arabia. In cabinets refrigerated to 315 degrees below zero, CRES maintains living skin cells and sperm samples representing more than 2,000 animals of 156 species, its insurance against doomsday in the animal world. But San Diego's zoo frustrated photographer Bob Cameron: from the air, its thick trees hide most of its inhabitants. The zoo is also a superb, semi-tropical horticultural park.

These rolling hills about 25 miles north of downtown San Diego, reminiscent of the uplands of Kenya, are home to 2,600 free-roaming animals. The San Diego Wild Animal Park is an 1,800-acre preserve developed in the San Pasqual Valley by the nonprofit Zoological Society of San Diego, which also manages the San Diego Zoo. Dedicated in 1972, the park fulfills a conservation role in propagation of endangered species. By nearly silent monorail, visitors wind through the park among the herds on the Wgasa Bush Line, a five-mile, guide-narrated tour. Curators of this park work with the Center for Reproduction of Endangered Species at the downtown zoo to improve and propagate troubled species such as cheetahs, gorillas, Chinese monal pheasants, and white rhinos. It was here that curators succeeded in hatching chicks of the California condor, once at the edge of extinction. There are thirty of the great birds now, and because of the work done here, some may soon be released in the wild.

About 700 solar collectors focus sunlight to make steam and generate electricity at a thirty-acre solar farm near Warner Springs. Funneled into mainline utility supplies, its peak capacity is enough to power the homes and businesses of about 3,000 residents. Built by LaJet Energy Co. in 1985, at a cost of $18 million, it is considered the largest privately-financed solar energy farm, and is owned by a partnership formed by Merrill Lynch.

(opposite) In settings such as Lake Poway, San Diegans are reminded that their homeland meets all the scientific criteria for desert and is sustained only by long aqueducts from northern California and the Colorado River. Lake Poway is a holding reservoir for imported water. It's also the prime recreation area for a town of 44,000 residents. With dry and barren hills rising behind it, Lake Poway, stocked with trout, has become a 400-acre recreation area with a fleet of 75 boats. Before water from the Colorado River reached Poway by aqueduct in the 1950's, there was no lake, no trees or lawns, and few residents.

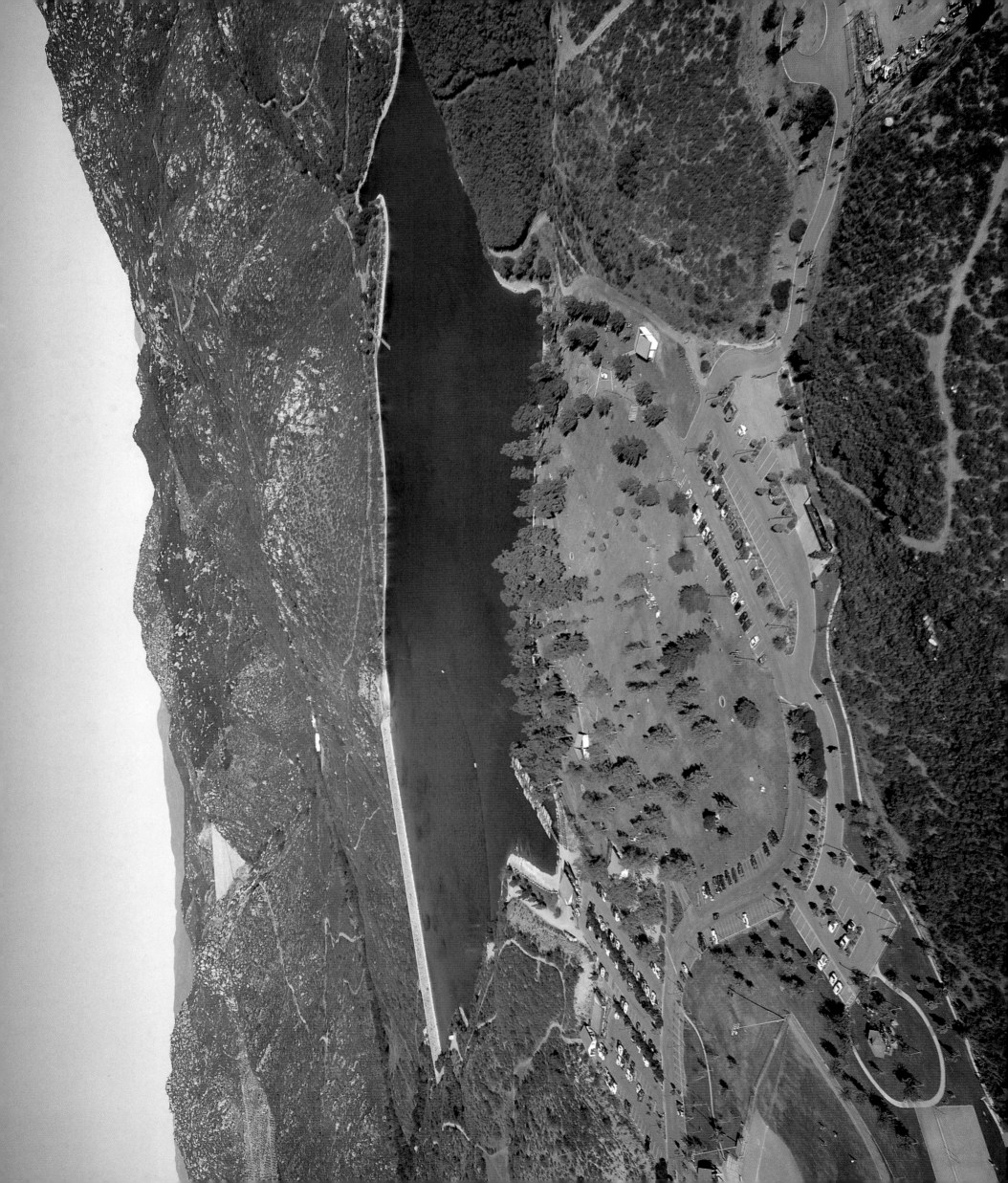

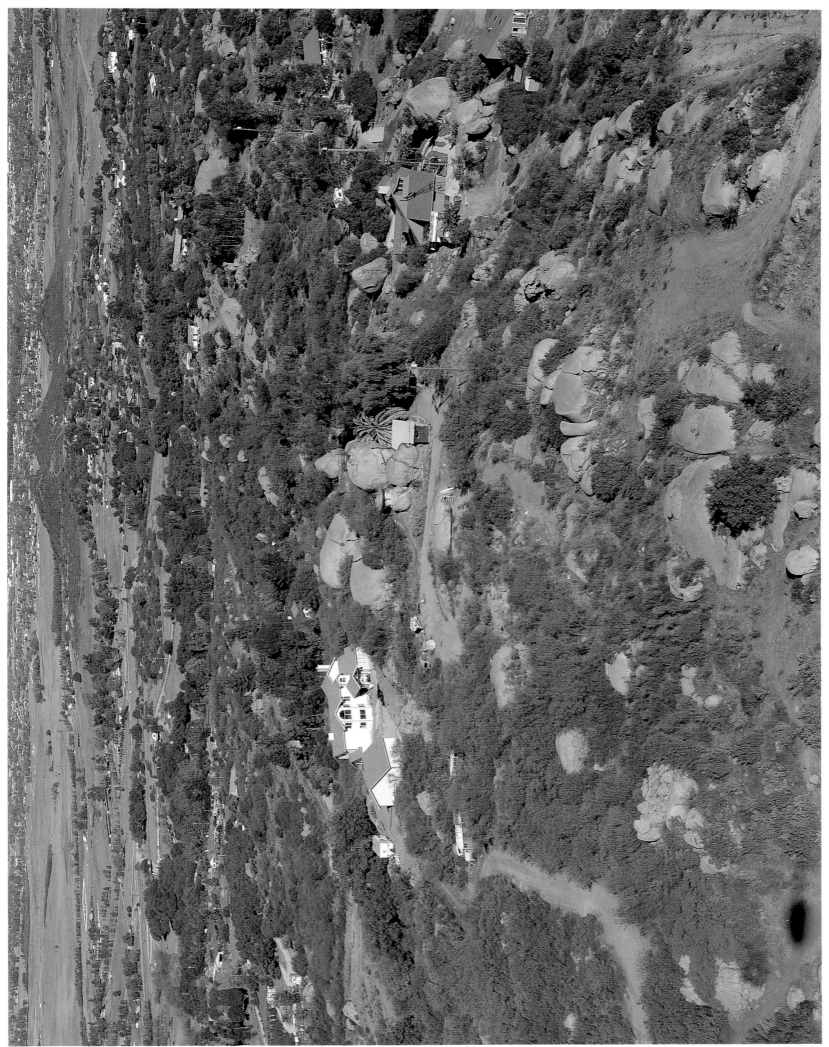

Geologists say San Diego County has an extraordinary diversity of earth forms. House-sized boulders dominate landscapes in several areas of the back-country, as in this range of hills between Mount Woodson and Ramona. The prizefighter Archie Moore trained here for defenses of his light-heavyweight title, and a nearby county road is named for him. A camellia farm occupies an oak-shaded valley above an underground stream. Increasingly, big homes are being built among the big rocks.

(opposite) Some 25,000 native Americans live in San Diego County. Fewer than 5,000 of them remain on the 18 Indian reservations that were set up in arid, inland areas between 1891 and 1913. This oasis surrounds a 19th-century asistencia mission on Santa Ysabel tribal lands that continues to serve as a chapel. More than 100 tribes are represented in San Diego: the largest are the Cahuilla, Cupeno, Diegueno, and Luiseno. Few of them still speak their tribal language. The once-powerful tribal medicine man has all but disappeared. Mounting school dropout rates and health care problems plague reservation residents.

Ramona is a town of 33,000 residents, named for the heroine of Helen Hunt Jackson's 1884 novel. Its main street lined with stately eucalyptus trees, Ramona wavers between a doggedly rural stance and its emerging role as a bedroom community of urban commuters. Ramona was once known for its turkey ranches, more recently for its egg farms. Cattle ranches ring its easterly hills. On Saturdays, working cowboys stride through Ramona's Alpha Beta supermarket, its ice cream parlors, and its one movie house, built in 1948. The tiny Ramona airport is remarkably like those that dotted America half a century ago. But now there's serious talk of enlarging that airport and beginning commuter airline service.

(opposite) Despite a reasonably well-confirmed Indian curse, Warner Springs has served several generations of San Diegans as a mountainside resort. The Pacific Crest Trail winds through its 2,500 acres, about seventy miles northeast of downtown San Diego. Warner's, as it's known locally, is at 3,200 feet, within view of Palomar Mountain's observatory and at the foot of the county's highest peak, Hot Springs Mountain, a dry and sheer summit at 6,533 feet.

Escondido, about 25 miles north of downtown San Diego, is the North County metropolis, with about 100,000 residents in 1990. Not so long ago, Escondido was happy to claim the largest lemon-packing plant in California, and groves of citrus and avocados surrounded the city. Now it is the urban hub for communities whose residents are involved in education, research and development, health care, and high technology production lines. Golden Door, a pioneer among luxury health spas, is just north of Escondido. City Hall is at the bottom of this picture, adjacent to

the intersection of Broadway and East Valley Parkway. Grape Day Park, at lower left, was named in an era when Borra and Ferrara were proud local wines and thousands of acres of muscat grapes were harvested each fall. Tourism is a recent innovation. Escondido motels and hotels are the closest to the San Diego Wild Animal Park. The city is a convenient and thrifty basing point for tours of mountains, desert and coast.

132

Bright green groves of lemons and oranges still sweep across dun hills as they did in the years before World War II; they owe their continued existence to a system of aqueducts and reservoirs that spans hundreds of miles across desert and mountains to bring water to San Diego. At the top of this picture is Lake Hodges Dam, another holding basin for imported water that irrigates this grove, within sight of the spacious estates of Rancho Santa Fe.

Canyons help to give urban San Diego its sense of roominess. Unsuitable for homesites, they were parceled by survey as add-ons to adjacent residential lots. Picture windows have views down long north-south canyon slopes toward urban valleys such as the east-west Mission Valley, or to the harbor or sea. The Spruce Street suspension footbridge is a landmark of Bankers Hill, an area of stately homes built in the early 1900's. It links two lengths of Spruce Street across a deep canyon. Not far away is the First Avenue Bridge, which opened Bankers Hill to direct automobile traffic from downtown San Diego in the years just before World War I.

Dudley's Bakery is an insider's outing. At Santa Ysabel, an hour's drive from central San Diego over narrow roads. Dudley's is a reason to go to the country. Wonderful breads are baked here, an astonishing variety of breads: my choice is the Jalapeno, studded with startling shards of hot chili peppers. In spring and fall, customer lines at Dudley's can mean an hour's wait, even for the fanatics who make the journey by helicopter. This picture was taken in autumn: those are pumpkins for sale beside Dudley's. Just seven miles above, up a steep, winding grade, is Julian, a mile-high gold-mine town redolent of the brief and unrewarding San Diego County gold rush of the 1870s. It is tucked among pines, oaks, lilac, and thickets of red-barked manzanita. Hidden in the forests of this coastal mountain range are the second homes of hundreds of San Diegans.

(opposite) For many years, San Diego population doubled each decade. Builders thrived, and so did nurserymen who sought out rural acreage for growing fields. This nursery near Del Dios grows thousands of shrubs and mature trees that help take the blight of newness off instant communities carved out of ranchland. Its house plants provide indoor decoration. The wholesale nursery industry is unique: the only kind of farming that is actually fostered by local population growth.

Much of the eastern two-thirds of San Diego County's 4,000 square miles is unpopulated desert, unfarmed and little traveled. Anza-Borrego Desert State Park, the largest contiguous state park in the nation, extends for sixty miles north and south. The town of Borrego Springs fans out from the spokes of Christmas Circle. Winter population may reach 6,000; in midsummer, when temperatures soar to 120, fewer than half remain. Borrego Springs is known by visitors for its elegant resort, La Casa Del Zorro (the house of the fox), and for its spiffy state-operated park visitors' center.

(opposite) The major industries of the Southern California deserts are agriculture and golf. The man most responsible for desert golf was the golfer Johnny Dawson, who set out in 1949 to make Palm Springs a golf resort. Bankers scoffed. But Dawson had studied underground water supplies. He paid $9,000 down on a 270-acre ranch that became the famed Thunderbird golf club. Wells made the grass green; shaded electric carts kept golfers comfortable in the blazing heat. The first of several desert golf courses in San Diego County was the De Anza Desert Club at Borrego Springs, sustained by underground desert rivers like the ones Dawson found.

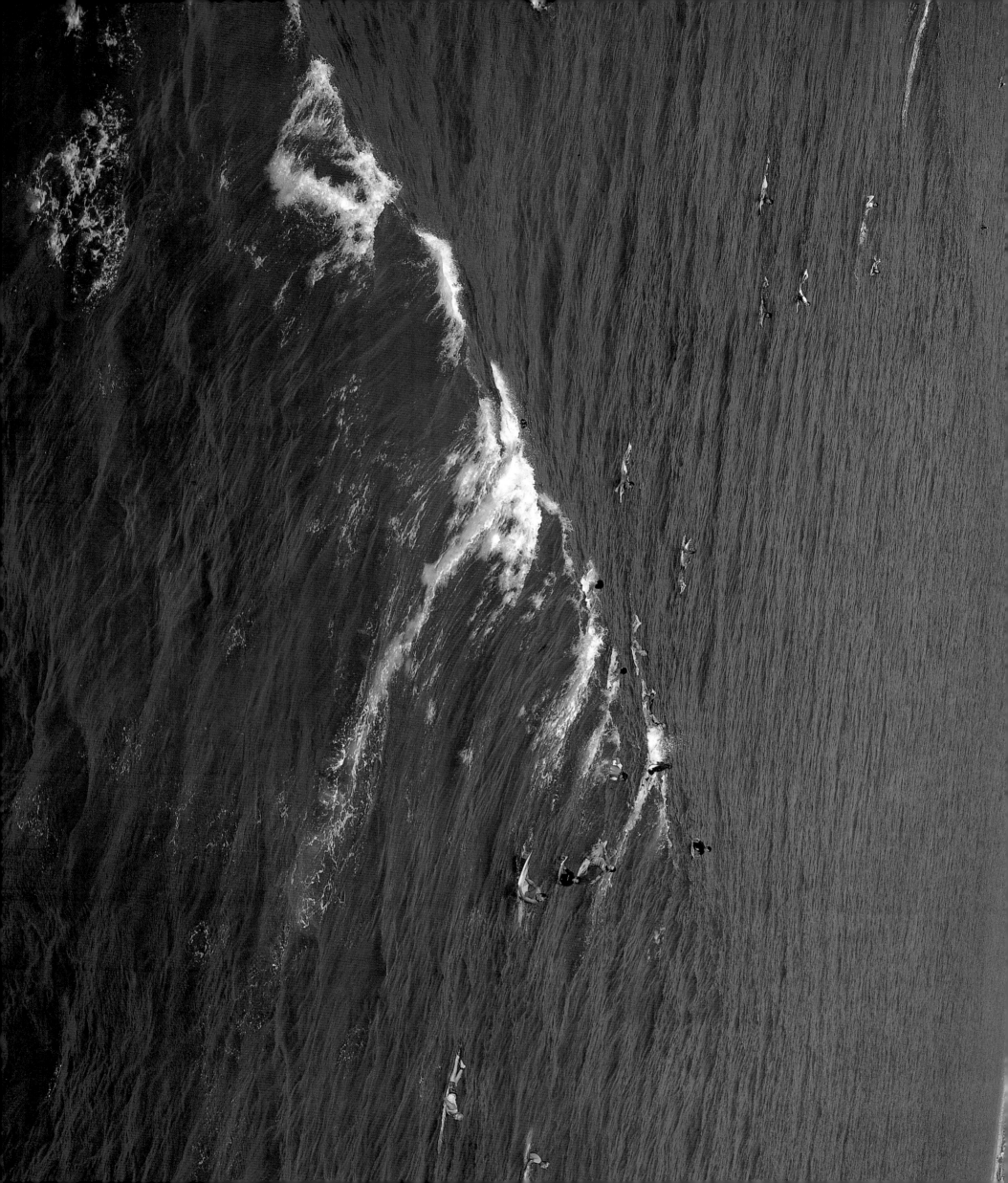

EVENTS

If it can be done under the sun and in the water, it's done in San Diego. The best-known surfing beaches are Windansea at La Jolla, Ocean Beach, Imperial Beach near the Mexican border, and San Onofre near the Orange County line at San Diego's north. Boating is a San Diego phenomenon: close to 50,000 boats are registered to San Diegans, and marinas like these in Mission Bay have waiting lists. Mission Bay is a seven-square-mile aquatic park created by San Diego planners in a conservation project launched in the 1950s. Mud flats had lain dormant near the center of the city ever since early explorers mired down in them and named the place False Bay. Dredging in recent decades has created pleasure islands and water channels zoned for varied water sports, for resorts, for picnicking and fishing. At bottom right are fishermen's bait barges.

Two San Diego expositions in Balboa Park, in 1915-16 and 1935-36, brought hundreds of thousands of visitors to San Diego. Some never left, and others returned to stay. The expositions established a superb architectural nucleus in the 1,400-acre park. Many of the neo-Spanish buildings designed by architect Bertram Goodhue have been replaced, but their style has been retained. Old or new, they house galleries, theaters, and museums that are the cultural heart of the city. One original structure, the California Tower, is a landmark seen through the right-side windows of airliners coming in to Lindbergh Field. It rises above the Museum of Man. Close by is the Old Globe Theatre, a widely regarded regional theater complex. The Old Globe has won its own Tony Award in connection with its continuing stream of Broadway-bound plays and musicals.

(opposite) The Natural History Museum in Balboa Park, the oldest scientific institution in Southern California, has concentrated since 1874 on regional phenomena that have made San Diego a jumping-off point for curators. The museum contains 8 million specimens. Its hall of desert ecology probes mysteries of the nearby Anza-Borrego Desert State Park. Its whale-watching expeditions take members hundreds of miles down the Pacific coast of the Baja California wilderness peninsula to lagoons where California gray whales complete their 5,000-mile migration from the Bering Sea to mate and calve.

The gentle arches of Balboa Park arcades and its gardens remind me of Seville and Granada, but then, of course, so does the San Diego climate. The central Prado of the park unfolds here: at top are the sculpture gardens and galleries of the San Diego Museum of Art and, at right, the adjacent Timken Gallery. Among the forested canyons beyond the Museum of Art lies the San Diego Zoo, also a part of Balboa Park. The zoo is known for its diverse community of creatures. But to horticulturists it is a rare collection of semi-tropical plants and trees, a forest so impenetrable from above that it frustrated even the inveterate Bob Cameron. Hidden beneath that foliage at far right is the zoo's Center for Reproduction of Endangered Species. Picture at right shows Starlight Bowl, the site of summer musicals.

Thoroughbreds run at the Del Mar racetrack from July through Labor Day, drawing cheery horse lovers from Texas and the Midwest who manage to make a vacation of the meeting. Summer rents soar in the beach communities from La Jolla to Oceanside. The racetrack is the site of the County Fair in July and of special events like the circus performance beneath this colorful tent.

Ballooning has become a year-round adventure above the coastal hills behind Del Mar. As many as twenty balloons can be seen soaring on weekend afternoons, picking up the late glint of the setting sun. Swim meets like this one (right) are commonplace in the seaside city that produced the great Channel swimmer Florence Chadwick.

Sea World, a marine entertainment park, opened in Mission Bay in 1964. With more than three million visitors a year, it has become a rival attraction to the San Diego Zoo. A solid base of animal research underlies the showbiz of Sea World and facilitates its role as breeder. Its killer whale shows, produced around the astonishing Shamu and Namu whale family, are among the most popular animal acts in history; anyone who has ever been kissed on the cheek by a whale remembers it. Dolphins and penguins are equally intriguing residents of Sea World. I spent an afternoon with Sea World's 300 penguins on their own ice blocks, and felt like a privileged guest in a dressy club. Sea World has recently diversified into non-nautical Americana: the City Streets musical pageant is staged in the arena at left.

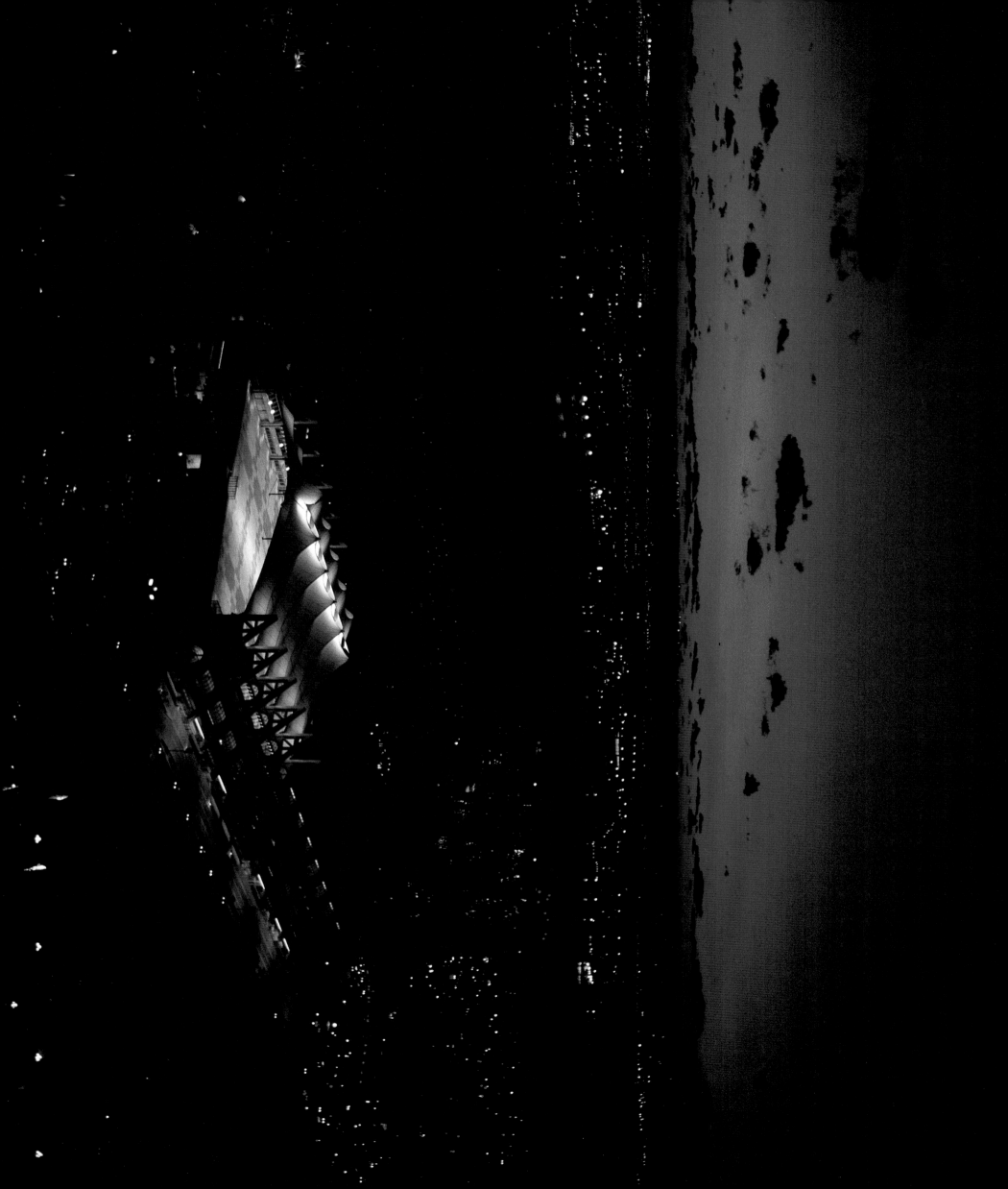

With about 35,000 students, San Diego State University is much the largest of San Diego educational institutions, and among the several largest in California. Traditionally it has had the closest community ties of any San Diego campus. Founded in 1897 as a normal school for teacher training, it was moved to an East San Diego mesa in 1931 and attached to the state college system in 1960. University status was accorded in 1971. Older campus structures are in the neo-Spanish mission style, newer ones in the institutional block fashion of mid-century. With a Donal Hord sculpture of Montezuma as campus mascot, students call themselves Aztecs. Bachelor's degrees are granted in 71 areas, master's in 55, and doctoral degrees in six. To cope with regional population growth, two other campuses have been established in Imperial County to the east, and in San Diego's North County at San Marcos.

(*opposite*) As dusk falls on San Diego, lights sparkle in the dry desert air, relieving the dusty, sometimes faded look of a land with perpetual sunshine and too little rain.

It was just what San Diego needed at a time of economic recession: In 1967, soon after *Time* had labeled San Diego a "bust city," a bargain $27 million sports stadium gave San Diegans a chance to call themselves a big-league city. It became the home of the Padres baseball club, which in 1984 made its way at this stadium to a World Series, and of the Chargers football club. The Chargers are still in quest of a Super Bowl, but the Bowl game came to this stadium in 1988 without the home-town team present. San Diego Jack Murphy Stadium carries the name of a former San Diego Union sports columnist.

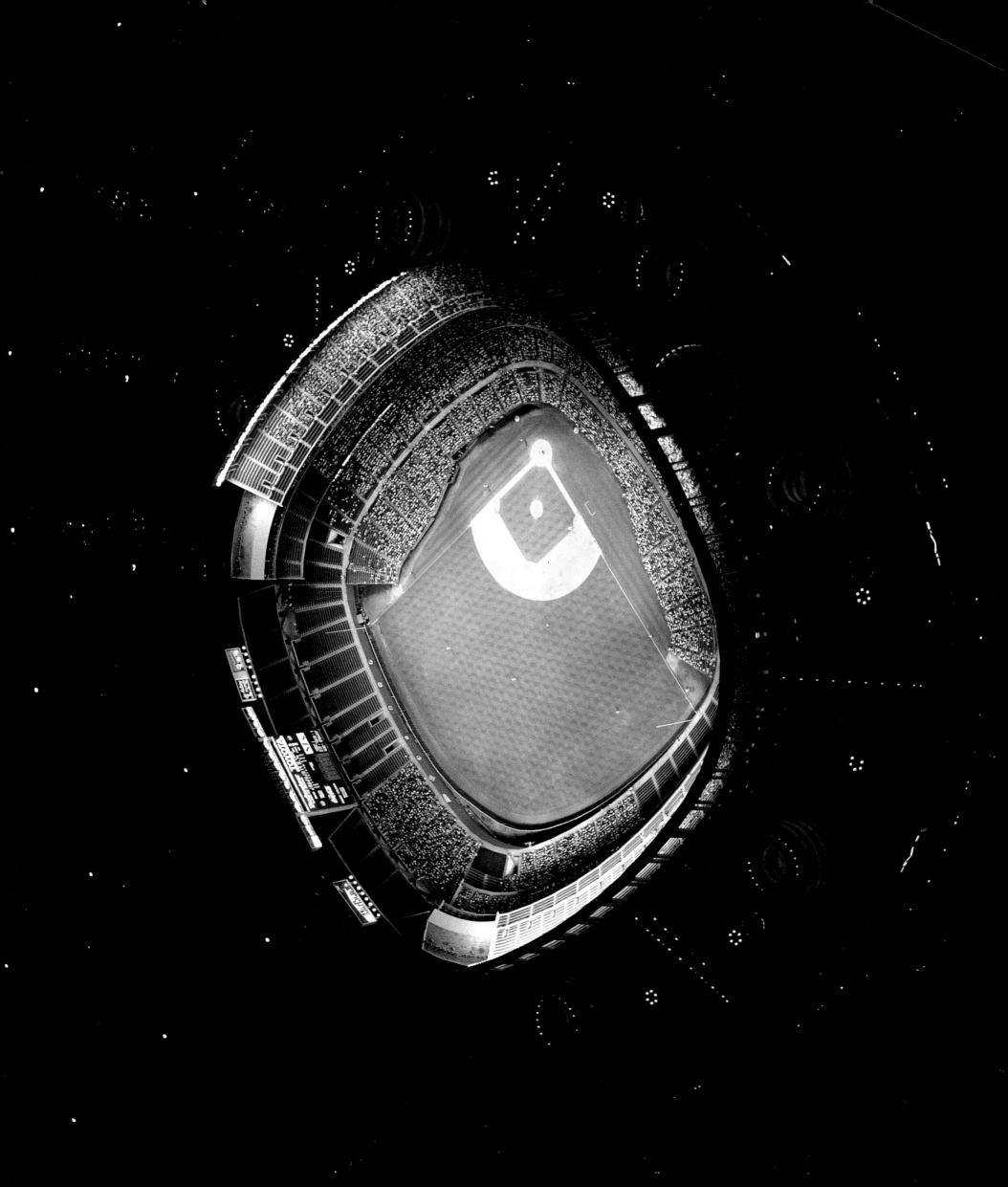

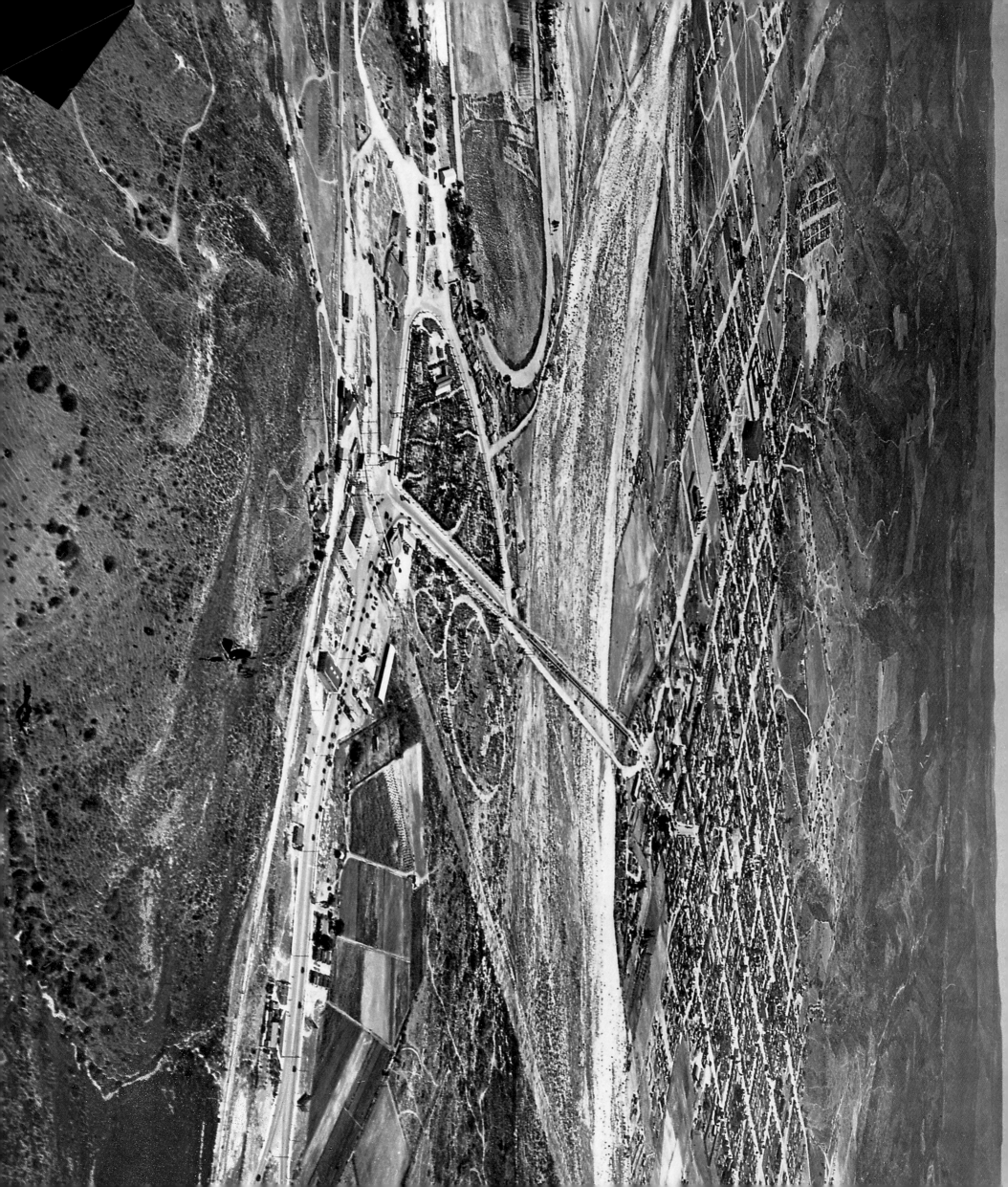

TIJUANA

The two largest cities along the nation's 1,950-mile border with Mexico are San Diego and Tijuana. They have a combined population of about four million. San Ysidro, where these two contiguous cities meet, is the busiest border crossing in the world. In 1934 (left), Tijuana was a town of fewer than 20,000, and illegal migration had not yet made this border a nightly battlefield. Now hundreds of U. S. Border Patrol agents, in steel-screened vehicles they call "war wagons," in helicopters and on motor bikes, seek nightly to intercept some of the hundreds who cross *La Linea* to seek work in *El Norte*. At other hours, legal commuter traffic between the two big cities clogs the 24 northbound lanes (bottom, right) where U. S. customs and immigration officers patrol. In the photograph at right, Tijuana extends from those lanes to the top of the picture, including the flood control channel that slashes across the city. Tijuana struggles with little hope to provide services for hundreds of thousands of Mexicans who come here from other states to seek jobs in some of the 450 assembly plants called maquiladoras, or to cross the border illegally in hope of higher wages. All seek escape from Mexico's continuing economic crisis.

For this picture, Bob Cameron positioned himself above the Pacific surf, just off the southwest corner of the United States, looking eastward down a straight and very distinct border where Tijuana joins San Diego. The seaside saucer just south of the border is one of Tijuana's two bullrings, the sites of ritualistic *corridas* on summer Sundays. Downtown Tijuana is three miles inland from the sea. Between are rolling hills that have become thronged *colonias*, neighborhoods of cluttered housing and dusty streets. Tijuana is a remote outpost of the national government at Mexico City, 1,400 miles away. Jobs, customs, and supply routes bring Tijuana and San Diego closer. Academicians who study the future of the Pacific Basin suggest the linkage of cheap Mexican labor and Yankee capital on this border sets up industrial and business potentials similar to those in Hong and Singapore.

(*opposite*) One of many anguishing ironies of this international border is the Soccer Field, a barren, eroded hillside that has been the scene of awful, repetitive violence: robbery, rape, and murder. The victims have been migrants, most of them native peasants from Mexico's interior, carrying their life savings as they seek by night to cross illegally from Tijuana, in the background, into San Diego. The criminals are most often young, drug-driven Mexican thugs exploiting this human river. By day, this slope continues to serve as a soccer field. Many have used the field as a metaphor for the tragedies of this border. It was the locus of Joseph Wambaugh's 1984 book about border crime, *Lines and Shadows*. As a writer for the *San Diego Tribune*, Jonathan Freedman won the Pulitzer Prize in 1987 for editorials centering on the Soccer Field and related immigration affairs. Freedman adopted the Mexican name for the Soccer Field: El Cañon de los Muertos: Canyon of the Dead.

160

ACKNOWLEDGMENTS

Alan Kappmeier of Accuracy Helicopter piloted the magical platform from which Bob Cameron made these photographs. He was guide, scout, and critic. "If we're lucky, the control tower will give us forty seconds over the Zoo," he said one afternoon, as airline jets rumbled down in their glide path beside us. His guess was on the button. His savvy in the air above San Diego has been acquired through years of piloting visiting photographers, land buyers, shopping mall builders, private detectives, and random sightseers. "You just took the prototypical view of Coronado Bridge," he told Bob Cameron one day. Cameron bristled but kept quiet. The photograph is not in the book.

When all the photographs were chosen, I needed more hours with Alan Kappmeier and a Thomas Brothers Guide to be certain where some of them had been made. If errors remain, it is the fault of the text writer. I've lived in San Diego for years. Cameron is from out of town.

For helping me to reduce the risk of dispute and error, I thank Dwight Donatto, Al JaCoby, Dulcie Molyneux, Bob Witty, Alison DaRosa, and especially my wife Judith Blakely Morgan, whose many roles include that of my favorite editor. Scores of San Diego friends pitched in with piles of fact and gossip about places and institutions pictured in Above San Diego, and I thank them all.

Jane Olcug Kristiansen designs Bob Cameron's books with sly understanding and sensitivity. She manages photographer and writer in an engaging variety of ways.

When his writer began to produce rather more words than expected, Bob Cameron did not display any of the peevishness that writers attribute to photographers and publishers. He was altogether gallant, both above San Diego and on the ground. His only regret, so far as I know, is that he was unable to photograph a bullfight from above Tijuana. He does not know how little he missed.

Neil Morgan

Page 2. Here in the nation's southwest corner, generations grew up with a sense of remoteness that had roots in the nineteenth-century American frontier. Railroad builders scorned San Diego as a cul-de-sac. To its south is the long, desert peninsula of Mexico's Baja California, much of it still wilderness. At the west is the Pacific: steep and barren mountains form a wall in the east. To the north sprawls a different kind of barrier, Los Angeles. Sea and harbor afforded San Diego its first thoroughfare. When the air age glimmered, grateful San Diegans rushed to give it a home, first with the advent of jets, the city burst out of isolation. At the Aerospace Museum in Balboa Park, the place of honor goes to an aircraft made in San Diego for the Navy, Convair's PBY Catalina seaplane. PBY pilots wrote a stirring early chapter of World War II in slowing the Japanese advance through the South Pacific. This museum roundhouse was the Ford Building in the 1935 California Pacific International Exposition; the automaker's V-8 insignia is preserved beneath the PBY tail.

Page 3. Children's Pool is one of the classic ocean beaches of a classic resort town. It lies within a sheltering arc of sandstone and concrete near the heart of "the village," a phrase still used by La Jollans since before it became a world playground. La Jolla is a suburb, dependent on San Diego for water and for protection from fire and crime, but La Jollans still talk of declaring independence from the city. The U.S. Postal Service humors La Jollans with their own postmark. Real estate agents insist that the name means tens of thousands of dollars more in the sale of a large home. Miles of Pacific Ocean beaches draw visitors to La Jolla, and many of them have come back to stay.

Page 4. San Diego is an urban world of water. The graceful arc of Coronado Bridge soars over San Diego Harbor, linking the mainland with Coronado, with the North Island Naval Air Station, and with the Silver Strand, a sandy hook of land that leads south to Mexico. About ten miles offshore, in Mexican waters, the Coronado Islands offer rocky haven to gulls and sea lions and a lighthouse keeper, and provide leeward shelter to fishermen.

Page 5. Just to the north of Tourmaline Beach is Windansea Beach. The contemporary novelist Tom Wolfe adopted La Jolla's Windansea Beach as the locus for "The Pumphouse Gang," one of his early explorations of American social mores. Then, as now, Windansea is all about surfing. Its waves often crest far out from shore and roll in ponderously gathering force and giving surfers the sustained power that allows them to test their limits. The waves finally break at the foot of some of La Jolla's most elegant homes.

Jacket photos: Cabrillo National Monument is near the southern tip of Point Loma, the arm of land that forms the west side of San Diego Bay. In 1542 Juan Rodriguez Cabrillo landed in the bay, the first European to visit this coast. The statue of Cabrillo seen on the jacket cover was donated by Portugal to California in 1949. Originally intended for San Francisco, it was diverted to its present site in San Diego. The old lighthouse seen on the cover was first lighted in 1855. The present lighthouse, just above water's edge, is seen on the back cover. It began operation in 1891. The top of Point Loma, about 400 feet above sea level, is a favored site for watching the midwinter migrations of California gray whales between the Bering Sea and Baja California lagoons.